GREAT WAR BRITAIN

HULL & THE HUMBER

Remembering 1914–18

GREAT WAR BRITAIN

HULL & THE HUMBER

Remembering 1914–18

SUSANNA O'NEILL

Dedicated to my grandparents,
with love

First published 2015

The History Press
The Mill, Brimscombe Port
Stroud, Gloucestershire, GL5 2QG
www.thehistorypress.co.uk

British Library Cataloguing in Publication Data.
A catalogue record for this book is available from the British Library.

ISBN 978 0 7509 6003 8

Typesetting and origination by The History Press
Printed and bound in Malta, by Melita Press.

CONTENTS

Timeline   6

Acknowledgements   9

Introduction   11

1   Outbreak of War   15

2   Preparations at Home   34

3   Work of War   53

4   News From the Front   70

5   Keep the Home Fires Burning   99

6   Coming Home   119

    Postscript: Legacy   137

Endnotes   152

About the Author   156

Bibliography   157

TIMELINE

1914

26 June

King George V opens new dock in Hull

28 June

*Assassination of Archduke
Franz Ferdinand in Sarajevo*

4 August

Great Britain declares war on Germany

*At the Hull Infirmary two wards
are set apart for war casualties*

23 August 1914

Battle of Tannenberg commences

1 September

Recruiting begins at 10 a.m. for Hull Pals

6 September

*First Battle of the Marne

Hull recruitment moves to the City Hall*

19 October

First Battle of Ypres

9 December

*Reckitt's VAD hospital
admits first patients*

1915

25 April

Allied landing at Gallipoli

3 May

*Seven Hull trawlers sunk by
German submarine attacks*

7 May

*Germans torpedo and
sink the Lusitania*

12 May

*Nearly forty Lusitania
survivors arrive in Hull*

31 May

*First German Zeppelin
raid on London*

6 June

First Zeppelin attack on Hull

7 June

Anti-German riots flare up in Hull

1 July

*6th Service Battalion (EYR) sail
from Avonmouth for Gallipoli*

28 August

*Funeral procession of E13
submarine victims through Hull*

8 December

*10th Battalion of EYR
sent to Egypt*

20 December

*Allies finish their evacuation of
and withdrawal from Gallipoli*

1916

4 January

*The Grimsby Chums
embark for France*

24 January

*The British Government
introduces conscription*

8 February

*1st Hull Heavy Battery sets
sail for East Africa*

21 February

Battle of Verdun commences

31 May

*Fifty-eight Hull men die at
the Battle of Jutland*

4 June

Brusilov Offensive commences

1 July

*Ninety-one Hull men die on the first
day of the Battle of the Somme, which
claims 57,000 British casualties*

13 November

*247 Hull men die attacking
the village of Serre*

18 December

Battle of Verdun ends

1917

	9 April *Battle of Arras*
3 May *139 Hull Pals die at Oppy Wood*	
	18 June *King George V visits Hull*
31 July *Third Battle of Ypres (Passchendaele)*	
	20 August *Third Battle of Verdun*
26 October *Second Battle of Passchendaele*	
	20 November *Battle of Cambrai*
28 December *Hull Private Charles McColl executed for desertion*	

1918

	3 March *Russia and the Central Powers sign the Treaty of Brest-Litovsk*
21 March *Second Battle of the Somme*	
	15 July *Second Battle of the Marne*
18 July *1st Hull Heavy Battery posted to France*	
	8 August *Battle of Amiens, first stage of the Hundred Days Offensive*
27 September *Storming of the Hindenburg Line*	
	8 November *Armistice negotiations commence*
9 November *Kaiser Wilhelm II abdicates, Germany is declared a Republic*	
	11 November *Armistice Day, cessation of hostilities on the Western Front*

1919

26 May *The remaining Hull Pals return home*	

ACKNOWLEDGEMENTS

There are many people to whom I would like to extend my thanks, for their help and input towards this book. I would specifically like to mention all the lovely people who welcomed me into their homes and shared the stories and memorabilia of loved ones with me. I felt very privileged to be party to their memories, letters, photographs and also their kind hospitality. So, thank you Kath and Dorothy Ellis for the detailed accounts of your grandfather's war; Alan Duckles for the stories of your father and family and for sharing with me the letters between your parents; Pat Bratton for the touching tales of your uncle; Dave Carrick for the stories of your great-uncle; Julie and George Bleasby and family for your fascinating tales and extensive memorabilia of family members in the war; Shelia Burr and family for the tragic accounts of your granddad and uncle, and for allowing me to use your moving poetry; Keith Burley for the information about your uncle and your kind support; Margaret and Harold Hardcastle for trusting me with so many precious letters; Andrew Winfield for the stories of your great-granddad; Mr and Mrs Carr, who have recently celebrated their Golden Wedding, for sharing your lovely keepsakes; Heather Littlejohn for your granddad's story and the minesweepers information; Mrs Collins for your kindness and family history; Lilian Rudd for the family information you shared with me, and also my great-auntie Dorothy, it was lovely to spend the time with you, getting to know a bit more about my own family history.

Every story, photograph and artefact gave me inspiration for this book and I only wish I had more space to include everything!

I would also like to extend my thanks to Charles Dinsdale, an invaluable fountain of knowledge about the Great War. Thank you for your precious time, help and inspiration.

My thanks go to Hull Museums for allowing me access to their brilliant archive of First World War photographs and Caroline Rhodes, Collections Curator, for your time and patience while I searched through them.

Thank you Martin Taylor, City Archivist, for your help and contacts, and the Hull History Centre for your interest and information.

Thank you to James Burton and the *Hull Daily Mail* for publishing my plea for local stories, without which this book could not have been written.

Thank you to Reckitt Benckiser for allowing me on to their premises to take photographs of the fountain and roll of honour, and thank you to Andrew Hersom for organising this opportunity and accompanying me.

Thank you to the Hull Carnegie Heritage Centre and to Steve and Hilary Manners for your time and help with information.

I would also like to thank The History Press and Matilda Richards for choosing me to write such an important book. It has been an honour and I am proud to have played my part in remembering the brave men and women of Hull from the First World War. My thanks also extend to the countless other authors and researchers who have written about this momentous war. I strongly urge readers to read the full version of the books I reference.

Last, but certainly not least, my thanks go to Judy and Arthur O'Neill, for your continued support, encouragement, ever-ready ear and valued proofreading.

INTRODUCTION

Early twentieth-century Britain, the greatest empire in the world, was the most technologically advanced nation on earth. Known as the 'empire upon which the sun never sets', we had unparalleled wealth and although there was widespread poverty and destitution within the working classes, Britons were proud of their country, loyal to their monarch. There existed such a powerful sense of duty and honour that the people of Britain were willing to fight, and die, for King and Country.

Louis Burton, Army Service Corps. (Courtesy of the author's great-auntie Dorothy)

There was true community spirit with strong family ties and reliance on each other. Without television or radio, art and poetry were the norm. Stories were recounted, music and sing-alongs plentiful and, of course, drinking with pals.

Life was hard for the working classes. In the great port of Hull, trawler fishing played a big part, but it was tough and dangerous work, with many lives being lost. Hours were long and arduous, the men having few rights or protections. These trawler men, along with their ships, were requisitioned in the First World War and thousands were killed whilst engaging in the perilous occupation of minesweeping to keep the seas clear for transport and food passage. These, along with the thousands of Pals who lost their lives, caused a gaping hole in the population of Hull.

The average man in the early 1900s was no taller than 5ft 6in, with a 34in chest. Average life expectancy was mid-forties but families were large and had to be supported. Thus working life began at a young age, extended education being reserved for the middle and upper classes. Malnutrition and rickets were common, with poor diets, cold houses and unclean living conditions. When war was declared and recruiting commenced, the chance of travel, of a clean set of clothes, regular meals, exercise and adventure proved very appealing to the young men of Britain who, believing it would all be over by Christmas, joined up in their thousands.

While the male youth of Hull were being trained and sent to fight, the womenfolk took over major roles, previously reserved for men. Communities rallied together, supporting each other when loved ones were lost and homes were bombed. Volunteers flooded the makeshift hospitals, Rest Stations and the Special Constable police force, immersing themselves in fundraising for food parcels and Christmas Comforts. The war affected all

Claude and Harry Skelton. As can be seen from his right-hand shoulder, Claude (left) was in the East Yorkshire Regiment. Harry (right) was a lance sergeant in the Army Service Corps. The Imperial Service Badge above his right pocket shows he volunteered to go overseas right at the beginning of the war. (Courtesy of the author's great-auntie Dorothy)

aspects of life and this book is a small commemoration of the suffering, the bravery, the turmoil and the sacrifice that the people in and around Hull experienced during that war to end all wars.

During my research I have had the privilege of talking to family members of some of the heroic lads of Hull that fought in this terrible war. I wish to extend my thanks to these people for allowing me a snapshot of their families' lives and I feel it a duty and honour to remember these brave souls through this book.

On a personal note, my great-auntie Dorothy Johnson, wife of my granddad's brother, told me that I had numerous family members involved in

One of the Dale's sons, my great-uncle. He was a signaller in the war. (Courtesy of the author's great-auntie Dorothy)

My great-grandfather Frank Johnson, top right. (Courtesy of the author's great-auntie Dorothy)

My great-great-uncle Arthur Harvey Burton, quartermaster and 1st class gunner. (Courtesy of his daughter, the author's great-auntie Dorothy)

the war. Her stepfather, Arthur Harvey Burton, born in 1887, was in the Royal Navy and was involved in the Battle of Jutland. He was a 1st class gunner and quartermaster on HMS *Lydiard*, a Laforey class torpedo boat destroyer, and his brother, Louis, was in the Army Service Corps. She also had three uncles on her mother's side who served. Claude and Arthur Skelton (who later opened the Hull Skelton Bakeries) joined the East Yorkshire Regiment and Harry Skelton was a lance sergeant in the Army Service Corps, whose barracks were in Walton Street, where the KC Stadium now stands. Later he was promoted to sergeant and served in France with the 50th Northumbrian Division. My grandfather's father, Frank Johnson, was a Royal Engineer, one of seven children. His wife, Alice Dale, was one of eight. Of the four boys in her family, two – Bert and Will – never returned from war.

Susanna O'Neill,
2015

1

OUTBREAK OF WAR

'Start of the European War. We deeply regret to state that Germany has declared war against Russia.' This was the headline of the *Hull Daily Mail* on 2 August 1914.

Following the assassination of Archduke Franz Ferdinand of Austria on 28 June 1914, all eyes had been scanning the newspapers, anticipating the outbreak of a war, and expectations were fully confirmed on 4 August when Britain entered the conflict. With this declaration came change for every man, woman and child, and a grim legacy of loss to be borne.

News came that troops were being mobilised and certain aspects of everyday life were changing already. 'Even the music halls are affected by the war', cited the *Hull Daily Mail* on 4 August. 'The Three Aeros, trapeze artists, were to appear at the Palace last evening, but could not keep their engagement as they had been called for military service.' The North-Eastern Railway reported it was withdrawing all excursions from 4 August. Concerns were expressed about the arrival of wheat, flour and sugar, and as early as 3 August 1914 the newspaper suggested that the people of Hull should start to become more vigilant with regards to waste, as the Germans were detaining trading ships and halting supplies to our port. 'Waste of every kind, especially food and fuel' was to be curbed. 'Petrol particularly should not be recklessly used.' Fruit and vegetable supplies were

> In 1887 Hull became one of the biggest fishing ports in Britain, providing food for a third of the country. Industry grew around imported commodities but the majority of the population lived in poverty with poor health and squalid living conditions.

also threatened: '… no steamer has left Hamburg, from whence a large quantity of fruit comes to Hull, since Wednesday.'

On the same date an early appeal was issued by Lady Nunburnholme for volunteers to come forward for training in first aid and nursing at the Voluntary Aid Headquarters, Peel House, No.150 Spring Bank. This was very far-sighted of her, as there were already eleven voluntary aid attachments in Hull and the surrounding area, but she insisted 'this number is quite insufficient for the calls likely to be put to them'. Her prediction was undoubtedly drawn from the fact that her husband was the Liberal Member of Parliament for West Hull and the Lord Lieutenant of the East Riding of Yorkshire and was instrumental in forming the Hull Pals battalions. In addition she asked for the people of Hull to donate what they could in the way of bedding, blankets, cutlery, pots, pans, soap, candles, candlesticks, matches, nightshirts, bed-jackets, hot-water bottles, baskets for boiled linen, bed pans and brandy!

In a special edition on the 5th, the *Hull Daily Mail* announced:

Declaration of war in Hull. All the long and anxious night large crowds paced the City Square and Whitefriargate, waiting for the final throw of the die. The momentous tidings broke out on the office front ere twelve o'clock midnight. Almost simultaneously copies of this journal were snapped up in the streets, and sold like hot cakes. Most people were hardly able in their excitement to read more than the fateful heading – WAR IT IS. Then deafening cheers broke out all along the line. Cheers were impartially given for France, England and Belgium.

The *Hull Daily Mail* also gave a rousing, patriotic statement, citing the reasons we had entered into the war and emphasised the obligation of every British family member to do their moral duty:

This country was left no alternative. Germany has violated the neutrality of Belgium, and she knew – she must have known – that this would be a cause of war with this country. Great Britain has not shirked her responsibility.

We all deplore a dire necessity, but we are compelled to face it. We must be faithful to treaties and to obligations, however costly, stern, and repellent the course forced upon us may be. The declaration of war between this country and Germany is rightly described … as one of the greatest events in history. His Majesty avowed his confidence that his army is capable of performing its heroic task. 'A country which defends itself gains the respect of all.' England will throw her 'preponderating fleet' against Germany. She is compelled to do so. Her position as a world-power is at stake. Germany is ambitious to take England's place, but she has placed herself in the wrong. Her policy and actions have been immoral.

And so it was, on 5 August 1914 the regular *Hull Daily Mail* broke the news:

War with Germany was declared last night, and the news was first announced in Hull from the 'Mail' office. A special midnight edition was published immediately, and the tremendous tidings, announced from the office window, evoked a great cheer from the large waiting crowd. Patriotic tunes were struck up with immense fervour. Hull was indeed stirred to its depths, as it has never been since the night of the Dogger Bank outrage trembled over the wires. 'Rule Britannia!' and 'Boys of the Bulldog Breed' – and even the 'Marseillaise' – were sung lustily, and were punctuated with loud cheers, with the question 'are we downhearted?' and the thundering negative reply. It was an unforgettable sight from above – this great concourse of several thousand singing men, not without a few women among them. The declaration of war arose automatically out of Germany's hostilities against Belgium.

It was not all celebrations in the city, however. The newspaper reported that on the same night war was declared 'a regrettable instance of rowdyism in Hull' was demonstrated.

Hull, like many other cities in Britain in the late nineteenth/ early twentieth century, had a sizable German immigrant population. A certain unrest concerning both immigrant and naturalised Germans had been growing towards the beginning of the war, country-wide, as the Anglo-German relations on an international scale began to deteriorate. Obviously with the declaration of war emotions ran high and Hull encountered its first anti-German hate crime. The case heard by the Hull Police Court in the morning, was that 'Victor Parker and Joseph Connell were jointly charged with breaking a plate glass window in Mr Hohenrein's shop in Waterworks street last night, and doing damage to the extent of £10.' Victor Parker told the court that:

> ... he was in Whitefriargate outside the newspaper offices, when the declaration of war between England and Germany became known. He was with his friend and both of them went to the Recruiting Office in Pryme street – he with the intention of joining the Navy and his friend the Army. When they got there, however, the Recruiting Office was closed for enlistment. He had intended to go there again at nine o'clock this morning. They afterwards went into Waterworks street, and noticed a crowd collected outside Mr Hohenrein's shop. He did not know Mr Hohenrein was a naturalised Englishman. He denied, however, throwing the stone at the window.

This was not the last anti-German rioting Hull experienced during the war, quite the opposite in fact, as news of the catastrophic figures of the dead at the front began to filter back home, as outrage for the sinking of the *Lusitania* struck and as people's homes and families were bombed by the Zeppelin raiders. Patriotism, tragedy, fury and propaganda had their part to play and Hull people were affected by them all.

The paper reported a similar incident in Grimsby on the 6th, concerning fisherman Arthur Patch who had been arrested for smashing a quantity of crockery at the shop of Mr Moller, a local German pork butcher, in Albert Street. In his drunken defence he is said to have stated, 'Well, he is a German!' The Mayor of Grimsby said this kind of behaviour was not to be tolerated and Mr Patch was imprisoned for fourteen days.

Emotions were running high in other areas too. Panic food buying and hoarding was the next hysteria to hit the streets of Hull, and it saw prices rise and supplies drop, until some semblance of order was restored, largely owing to the Retail Grocers' Association. 'They have done their best to resist panic-buying by declining to execute orders for unreasonable quantities and panic prices have been kept down.'

Hull also remonstrated against those thoughtless folk who were demanding gold from the bankers, to the ruin of the credit of the country:

Let it be understood that the man who goes to the Bank and obtains gold in excess of his legitimate requirements in order that he may hoard it up to meet possible emergencies is guilty of an act of the grossest selfishness. The meanness of the transaction is in no sense distinguishable from the act of one who, in the face of an anticipated shortage of food, proceeds to make extensive purchases in excess of his needs, thus protecting himself against possible inconvenience at the expense of his poorer neighbour who by stress of circumstances must live hand to mouth. If there is a shortage, let us all suffer alike.

Early preparations were already being put in place for possible casualties that might be brought to Hull. A meeting, held at Hull Guildhall, was attended by about a hundred of Hull's leading citizens. As the men were already engaged in war preparations, they were mostly ladies, including Lady Nunburnholme, Lady Sykes, Mrs Wilson and Mrs Reckitt. The crux of the meeting was to organise hospital accommodation for the sick or wounded as well as arranging various methods of transport to Hull. Reckitt's had promised beds and more had been secured at the Metropole Assembly Hall and the Waltham Street Schoolroom, the Baptist Schoolroom in Trafalgar Street and another in Quay Street. It was stated that there would be 'no dearth of nurses, as already many had volunteered their services. That morning alone there had been nearly a hundred applications. Some … were trained nurses and others were not.'

Although there were some people who urged for peace and negotiations rather than war, the general feeling in Hull in these early days was one of a general pulling together, of pride as well as anticipation, and the newspapers reflected this. One article, entitled 'How to be useful in war time', gave people encouragement as well as advice: 'First and foremost – Keep your heads. Be calm. Go about your ordinary business quietly and soberly. Try to contribute your share by doing your duty in your own place and your own sphere. Be abstemious and economical. Avoid waste. Do what you can to cheer and encourage our soldiers. Gladly help any organisation for their comfort and welfare.'

Chief Skipper William Jackson. (Courtesy of Heather Littlejohn)

Hull trawler men and their vessels played a crucial and often underrated role in the war. The fishing trade was badly hit when the navy commandeered the fishing fleet to be turned into minesweepers and most of Hull's many fish and chip shops closed.[1]

One Hull lady I met, Heather Littlejohn, told me that her granddad, Chief Skipper William Jackson, was an admiral. Born in 1880, in Norfolk, he moved to Hull around age 12. He carried on the tradition of his father and uncles by becoming a fisherman and then a fully qualified skipper by 1907. Heather showed me papers from the war, when William was recruited as skipper aboard a Hull trawler, the HMS *Gull*, which – like most of the fleet – was commandeered for the war. It was on this ship that he gained entry into the RNR Medal Book of Commendation. Later on he also commanded HE *Stroud*. As early as 1913 the lordships of the Admiralty visited Grimsby and studied how the trawler men handled their nets and the idea was set in motion to use the North Sea Fishing Fleets and their crews as minesweepers in the Trawler Division during the war. Just as the normal bank clerks, butchers, tailors etc. were unprepared for the harsh realities of war, so were the fishermen suddenly thrust into a military state, tasked with trawling for mines in enemy-infested waters. They were given temporary commissions, no real recognition for the dangerous role they undertook, but then this was a time of danger for everyone. William joined the Royal Naval Reserve on 26 October 1914 and was deployed in the Trawler Section for the whole duration.

Chief Skipper William Jackson. (Courtesy of Heather Littlejohn)

Another Hull lady's relative, Dorothy Ellis's father, Albert Beckett, was born in a workhouse in Fareham but ran away age 12 to join the sailing ships. He eventually worked on the *Brocklesby* steam ferry, which carried passengers across the River Humber between Hull and New Holland, along with the *Killingholme*. The *Killingholme* was torpedoed in 1916, with the loss of eighteen lives. At the start of the war both these ships were also requisitioned for Admiralty service and used as armed seaplane carriers. Built at Hull's Earle's Shipyard in 1912, these sister ships were fairly new at this time and

The population of Hull, estimated by the Hull Medical Officer of Health in 1912, was 283,000, rising from an estimated 186,292 in 1885 up to 291,118 in 1914. The number of houses in 1895 was 53,398, rising to 60,237 in 1906. For every 1,000 births in working-class homes in Hull, 124 died in infancy.

Chief Skipper William Jackson and the crew of the HE Stroud. (Courtesy of Heather Littlejohn)

because of their lower draught it was thought that they would be safer from mines or torpedo attacks than the trawlers. They had been designed to carry sheep, but their large open decks were adapted to be able to carry four Schneider seaplanes in the war. They were not built for open seas and did not fare well in rough weather but they had an important job of leading the planes to shoot down Zeppelin bombers. Dorothy and her daughter, Kath, showed me a copy of the log from the *Brocklesby* in August 1916 documenting Zeppelin sightings and the use of their seaplanes. Albert Beckett is believed to have been on board during this period. He also worked aboard the SS *Chicago*, travelling to New York in 1917, which was lucky, as this ship was torpedoed off Flamborough Head the next year, sinking within ten minutes. Albert's family believe he sailed on the SS *Port Augusta* after this, in early 1919, visiting the Pitcairn Islands, where he recounted that the islanders were not aware that the war was over.

Albert Beckett. In the left-hand photograph he is seen seated, after a few pints with his brother-in-law. As a joke they thought they would swap uniforms for the photo! (Courtesy of Kath and Dorothy Ellis)

Hull's income greatly relied upon its importation businesses. By 1913 Germany was shipping 763,206 tons of coal through Hull and trade with Germany accounted for 11 per cent of the total inward and outward tonnage. When war was declared all trade with Germany and her allies ceased.

Albert Beckett and the crew of the HMS Brocklesby. *(Courtesy of Kath and Dorothy Ellis)*

Dead man's penny sent to the family of Laurence Cyril Burley. (Courtesy of Keith Burley)

Hull man Keith Burley's uncle, Laurence Cyril Burley, joined up, becoming a 2nd class steward on the SS *Rhydwen*, in the Mercantile Marine Regiment, aged just 16. Both his brothers, William and Bernard, also fought in the war, Bernard serving in the 11th East Yorkshire Regiment. While his brothers both survived, Laurence was lost at sea on 18 April 1917, aged just 16. He drowned as a result of an attack by an enemy submarine. His heartbroken parents left him this message in the *Hull Daily Mail*: 'Not just today, but every day, Beloved, we think of thee. Until the brightest of all Easter days.'

The knock-on effect of the huge loss of recruiting men affected all aspects of life: agriculture, fishing, factories – even sport. The *Hull Daily Mail* reported on 5 August 1914 that Jimmy McIntosh, the captain of the Hull City Football Club, 'has been called to the Colours and leaves Hull at 12 o'clock to join the Highland Light Infantry'.

This was only the beginning. On 8 August, Lord Kitchener called for a new army of 100,000 men to reinforce the regular army. This, of course, increased dramatically the next year, to 600,000, and men flooded the recruitment offices, leaving gaping holes in all areas of life and industry.

The town was abuzz with talk of the war, and cinemas and theatres held rousing speeches to encourage men to join up. The *Hull Daily Mail* ran a piece on the 7th:

> Wilson Line Announcement. The chairman and directors of the Wilson Line wish it to be known that members of the staff who are desirous to volunteer for service can do so resting fully assured that their positions in the firm are secured to them. At the present the authorities are asking for unmarried men between the ages of 18 and 30.

Laurence Cyril Burley, 2nd class steward on SS Rhydwen. (Courtesy of Keith Burley)

The ball was rolling; young men felt the call, the desire and the responsibility to enlist:

> Sir, – Fourteen years have passed since the formation of the Hull Patriotic Rifle Club. Now is the time to see what that has led to. Should we not mobilise the whole of the rifle clubs of England? Let the call go forth from Hull once more. Let us now join again in the defence of our country, and the honour of the Empire. Let every skilled shot present himself for enrolment as a special rifle club brigade, and place ourselves under training and discipline ready to stand in the ranks with our Territorial Forces. The call to arms has come! Are the Rifle Clubs of England ready?[3]

HAROLD TESSEYMAN

The general consensus of feeling from the troops leaving to fight was one of duty, adventure and honour. They would miss those at home but had every expectation that they would see them again before long.

The following letter is from Harold Tesseyman, courtesy of Margaret Hardcastle, dated 28 November 1914:

> 3rd Reserve Heavy Battery, R.G.A., Sergeants' Mess,
> 'T' Lines, Avington Park, Winchester, Hants.

Dear old sports, just a few lines to let you know I am settling down fairly well here. I work my head & generally manage to get myself where most of the work is 'put out' & so far have had a very decent time. Am on medical inspection today & expect I shall be in category A & fit for active service, although I think I shall be here until well over Xmas & then get 4 days at home before going overseas. I had a decent time on leave only got very little time to myself or at home. I shall not go round & see anybody when I am on my overseas leave, but of course shall make an exception in your case. Felt a bit rotten as I steamed out of Paragon & saw you all waving, but I never seem to get homesick & a good job too, although of course I always like to come home & shall be glad when I come to stop. Have not been into Winchester yet as it is a good 4 miles from here & all uphill coming back but shall probably go down on Saturday all being well & have a look round. Well, 'nowt to tell ec'. Remember me to everyone not forgetting Babs & tell her that her uncle is always thinking about her & hoping she is a real good girl. Well, cheerio, yours to a • Harold.

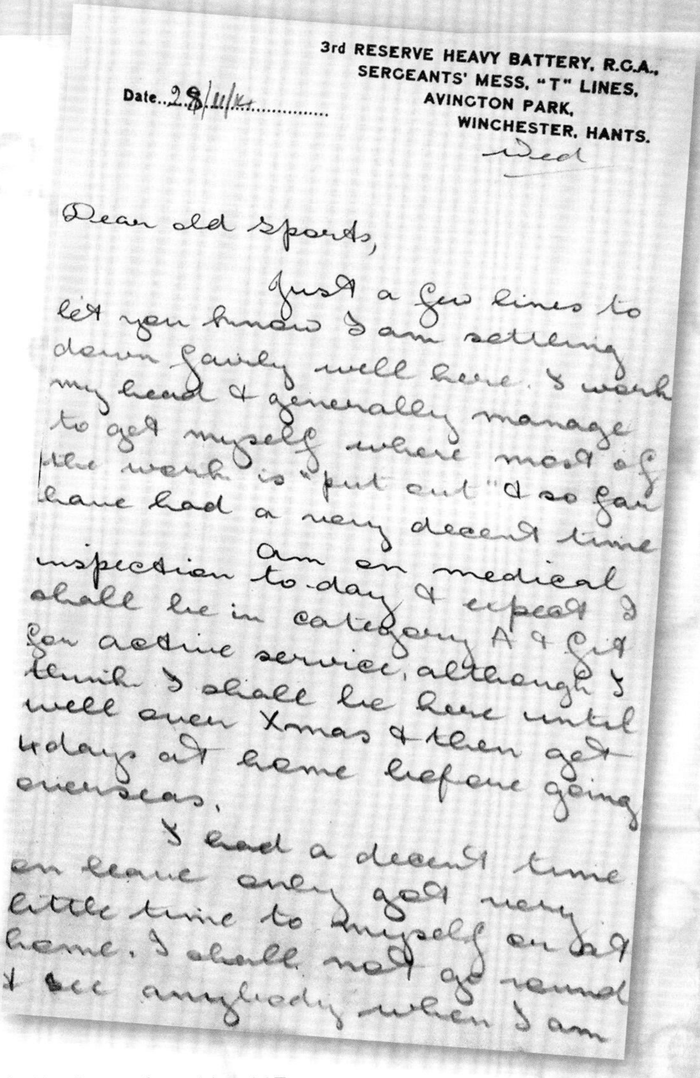

3rd RESERVE HEAVY BATTERY, R.G.A.,
SERGEANTS' MESS, "T" LINES,
AVINGTON PARK,
WINCHESTER, HANTS.

Date 28/11/14

Dear old sports,

Just a few lines to let you know I am settling down fairly well here. I work my head & generally manage to get myself where most of the work is "put out" & so far have had a very decent time.

Am on medical inspection to-day & expect I shall be in category A & fit for active service, although I think I shall be here until well over Xmas & then get 4 days at home before going overseas.

I had a decent time on leave, only got very little time to myself or at home. I shall not go round & see anybody when I am

Letter home from Harold Tesseyman,
28 November 1914. (Courtesy of Margaret Hardcastle)

The numbers of recruits rose especially quickly after the casualty figures from the first few battles began to filter through: Mons, Marne, Cambrai, Gallipolli. The tragic loss of so many young lives seemed to fire the resolve of others to take their places and carry on the fight.

Margaret Hardcastle was kind enough to allow me access to over fifty letters she has that were written by her two great-uncles, William and Harold Tesseyman, during their time in service during the war, addressed to her grandparents, Catherine Madge and John. Every letter sends kisses to their young niece, Babs, who was Margaret's mother, of whom both men were obviously very fond. William became a sergeant in the Royal Army Medical Corps (RAMC) of the East Yorkshire Regiment, enlisting in August 1914, aged 27.

The following is an early letter from William, it mentions that he has not gone abroad yet, so probably dates from late 1914:

William Frank Tesseyman, North Bay beach, Scarborough. (Courtesy of Margaret Hardcastle)

Sergeant Harold Tesseyman, 124th Hull Heavy Battery RGA, with letters he and William sent home. (Courtesy of Margaret Hardcastle)

34th Field Ambulance, 'a' Section,
Hillsboro Barracks, Sheffield.

My dear Madge and John,

I received your letter & also fine cake safely last night. Thanks very much for it. It is a grand one! I am quite settled down here in the Ramc, although it was much better at Grantham than here! The work here is very interesting although very creepy. We have to learn all about first aid, such as stopping bleeding and bandaging etc. We expect to go to the front soon after Xmas & shall be at these Barracks for about two months yet I expect. – I don't know when I shall get another pass, probably in three weeks time, so when I do, I will find time to come to see you. I am glad Babs is keeping well. – Well I must close now, as I have several letters to write yet!

Best love to Babs and all. Your loving brother Will.

Harold also joined up in 1914, becoming a sergeant, then an officer in the 124th Hull Heavy Battery RGA, 11th Hull Pals Battalion.

Within the first six months of the war 20,000 men from Hull had enlisted, this figure rising to over 70,000 by the end of the conflict.[4] Suddenly the streets of Hull were full of troops, the likes of which had never been witnessed before. The young men who had enlisted held their heads high with the pride of going to serve their country and the women they left behind were just as proud of them.

The *Hull Daily Mail* published a letter from the diary of a soldier's wife, expressing such sentiments:

> This evening the order has come for general mobilisation. For three days we have waited for it and now my heart swells. As I write I hear the band in the barracks. It plays the 'Marseillaise' – after our own National Anthem. Then come ringing cheers. I thank God I am the wife of a British officer and the mother of children who may some day feel this pride I now feel. It is my first experience of war. The grip in my heart is inevitable. Suppressed excitement in me is intense. All the pettiness of life sink to nothingness. My thoughts are one huge unexpressed prayer to my Maker. One tries to suppress individual thoughts. One feels them unworthy in this moment of tensity. The thoughts of fear shall never materialise. There will be work here for us women. The responsibility of our homes we now shall bear single-handed. Our trust we must carry out to the very utmost – the hysterical element must not be let in. It is a wonderful time for us to live through with laurels. I, for one, am truly thankful, and there must be many a soldier's wife who feels the same.[5]

This was quite a change in attitudes, as one soldier colourfully illustrated in the monthly journal of the East Yorkshire Regiment, *The Snapper*.

A few years back a soldier was —
Well, nothing much, to say;
How different is the story
That people tell to-day.
To those men who enlisted
Ere the Country went to war,
It must seem to them, it cannot be
The same world as before.

Before war clouds came o'er us —
See a soldier in the street:
See how he's get cold-shouldered
By everyone he'd meet.
They used to say that Tommy was
The scum of all the Earth;
To feed them like the Army did
Was more than they were worth.

One heard in many a household
If one son, heard the call,
'Don't let him join the Army,
'Twill be the lad's downfall.
The Army's full of failures —
Men, who refuse to work —
Disgraces to the Country,
Any decent job they'd shirk.'

Tommy never gave an answer
To those who slurred his name,
But quietly vowed, if given the chance,
He'd make them blush with shame.
They never hurt his feelings much —
He pitied, more than blamed —
He knew 'twas ignorance, of which
Some day they'd be ashamed.

'Twas not because he would not work
That Tommy served his King.
That was the tale he told the crowd
Who, at him, mud did sling.
Some people, will ask questions
In the manner of Paul Pry's,
Can they blame our gallant Tommy
If he pulled their legs with lies.

They seldom got a word of praise
Except 'twas from their King
Who knew their worth, and knew that they
Would give their lives for him.
His Majesty – God bless him! – knew
That they were game to die –
To give their lives, that Britain keep
The Union Jack on high.

God! how our Tommies answered them
At Mons – the Marne – Cambrai.
The Persian Gulf, Gallipolli,
In thousands, they did die;
They died that you, your children
Should never feel the shame
Of a defeat for Britain's Flag
Or slur on Britain's name.

'Take back those words! you people, who
At Tommy cast a slur;
'Twas not the British soldier –
'Twas you, that was the cur.
You should go on your knees and pray
To God, if God you own,
For those brave lads that died to save
Your Empire, and your home.[6]

How true these words were already when they were written towards the end of 1915, and yet there was so much more to come. Perhaps his poetic licence exaggerated the view of the common soldier before the war, but certainly at the outbreak of hostilities the consensus was that it was every able-bodied man's duty to fight. Little did the ordinary man – the bank clerk, the accountant, the teacher, the tram driver, the road sweeper – know of the realities of war. The glory and honour that the Empire had brought ill prepared the public for the actuality, as Anthony Babington highlighted:

> The 1891 Census showed that Hull had 906 German residents in its boundaries, many being pork butchers. On the outbreak of war, German residents in Hull were rounded up and kept aboard the Wilson liner *Borodino* in King George Dock – 300 were arrested.

Most of them had been impelled to join up through the most unselfish of motives – a resolute sense of duty or an emotional desire to serve their country in her hour of need. Many had neither the physique nor the temperament of the fighting man and still retained a visionary concept of warfare distorted by notions of chivalry and romance. Few of them at the moment of enlistment could possibly have predicted their reactions under fire or their endurance to the sights, the sounds and the stains of the battlefield.[7]

These brave lambs knew naught of the slaughter that awaited them.

2

PREPARATIONS AT HOME

The war was on. Preparations at home were immediately underway, especially the push to encourage the young men of Hull to join up. Recruitment was somewhat slow to begin with, theories suggesting that, because of censorship, all the news from the front seemed victorious. The indication was that the war was being won and would be soon over, so there was no rush to join up. However, with the bombing of Scarborough and the E13 submarine tragedy, and more authentic reports filtering through about the major losses at the front as well as stories of the German treatment of Belgian and French inhabitants, the men started to understand that they were needed.

10th Service Battalion in training, with armbands on show. (Courtesy of Hull Museums)

At Victoria Station the other day
Before the leave train got under way.
There hove in sight a bold T.A.,
Who, to put it politely, was a trifle 'tight',
And needed support both left and right.
It was, I grant, a deplorable sight,
But the point is: he got his train alright!

As I watched his somewhat erratic course
And thought with awe of his wild debauch,
Two smug civilians went tripping by,
And one nudged the other, and winked his eye:
The both of them smiled a contemptuous smile
As they paused to watch for a little while,
And writ all over them one could see –
'Thank God! I'm not such a one as he.'

Have you ever thought, oh, civilian, bold,
What it's like in Flanders now it's turning cold?
Have you ever stood on a pitch-black night
Watching the Bosch send up his lights:
A'listening to the bullets' thuds,
Wondering if your feet are 'duds'?
Or lived in a sort of glorified drain,
And felt persistent rheumatic pain?
Had you done those things you would understand,
And give all Tommies a helping hand.

Oh! Self-righteous civilian, with your face so smug,
You ought to have gone on your knees in the mud,
And thanked your God, if a God you own,
For the men who are willing to leave wife and home,
Going out fearless to face the unknown.[8]

Recruitment drives dominated the city and the demand for more soldiers was unavoidable. The old Pryme Street recruitment offices were seen as too drab and too small for the task and so the whole affair was moved to the Hull City Hall.

> *I see the fine drilling of men strong and willing,*
> *Who'll fight for the Empire we all love so well;*
> *The sight gives me pleasure, in depth beyond measure;*
> *My pen cannot write it, my tongue cannot tell.*
>
> *In dreams of the morning I see the day dawning,*
> *When justice and freedom shall bless every land;*
> *For this we are working, no struggle e'er shirking,*
> *For this we are taking our resolute stand.*
>
> *Many nations oppressed have called Britain blessed,*
> *Her arm has been stretched to their aid, not in vain;*
> *We tell the proud story of Britain's great glory –*
> *May God-inspired heroes her splendour maintain!*
>
> *All hail! day most glorious, when Britain victorious*
> *Continues in peace her great work for mankind;*
> *With record unblotted, and honour unspotted,*
> *High hopes are before her, achievements behind!*⁹

Armband issued to 4th Hull Battalion, before uniforms were available. (Courtesy of Hull Museums)

The City Hall was bedecked with colourful flags, posters and bunting and often the balcony was employed for the use of patriotic speeches, ringing out to the crowds below.

10th Service Battalion on parade in Hull. (Courtesy of Hull Museums)

Hull cinemas and theatres also threw open their doors for recruitment, allowing screens to show films which would inspire young men to join up and permitting their premises to be used for rousing recruitment speeches.

A large parade, one of many, was organised on 3 October around the city. This 4,000-strong march of new recruits attracted much public attention and hundreds turned out in enthusiastic crowds to cheer on the men whose battalions were identified by an armlet they wore, as no uniforms had yet been issued. One can only imagine the thrill of seeing hundreds of soldiers smartly marching past with the infectious sound of the band enticing onlookers to join.

Special treatment was offered to soldiers, encouraging more to sign up; 'Free Rides on Hull Trams' stated the newspaper.[10] 'By permission of the Lord Mayor … military in uniform will be allowed to ride for free in the tramcars. This is a special arrangement during the present crisis.' Special tramcars were also allotted for taking new recruits to the City Hall. These cars had been decorated with the flags of the Allies, to further stimulate patriotic fervour.

As early as September 1914, nearly 6,000 Hull men had joined the new army. The *Hull Daily Mail* offered the following figures: Wenlock Barracks 1,600, Pryme Street 800, Londesborough Barracks 400, Commercials 1,020, Tradesmen 1,020, Athletes 400, Hull Heavy Battery 120 and East Hull Depot 300.

WHAT WAR MEANS –
HULL LAD'S NOBLE LETTER

The following letter has been received from mechanician Joe Melady, on HMS *Defence*, in the Mediterranean, written to his mother at Newland, Hull:

HMS *Defence* –

Dear Mother, - I now take this opportunity of writing to you, hoping to find you in good health, as I am pleased to say I am myself at present.

I haven't had a chance to write earlier, and don't know when I will be able to send this, as of course you know we are at war, and we are working or watching day and night.

One would never dream what a terrible thing it is to be in a ship in time of war. We have had to throw everything over-board except a few things we left in Malta. We haven't even a table to eat our food stuff off, as all inflammable stuff, such as wood, and breakable things such as glass, cups, etc., must go, as lives would be lost through them breaking and flying round in action.

We are looking for a German battle-cruiser, the *Goeben*, and have orders to bring her to action at any cost and as she is a lot stronger and faster than us it will be a difficult task.

Dear mother, you must have courage, and trust in God, as I am myself, and always remember that, if disaster befalls us, I will die as you would wish me to, bravely.

If the sacrifice must be made, think that it is for the good of the country, and be resigned. Don't sit down and cry, but thank God you have reared sons who could, and would, do it, and have only one regret, that they couldn't do it twice.

When I come home again, I will be able to tell you all about it. I hope you are not having a bad time in Hull, and that you are all well, but I suppose the price of foodstuffs will have gone up.

Give my love to Nelly and Annie and Harry. Say that they mustn't expect any letters and that 'No news is good news'. If we meet the German, and get beat, you'll know about it before you receive this. So don't worry, and accept love from your loving son, Joe.

(Published in the *Hull Daily Mail*, 29 August 1914)

HMS Defence. *(Wikimedia Commons)*

After the initial slow start men were soon flocking to join up, Kitchener's stirring words for a 'New Army' finally hitting home, and relays of volunteer staff were needed to deal with the numbers. Thomas Sheppard declared that:

... the Hull Recruiting Office was looked upon by the War Office as one of the most successful and efficient recruiting offices within the kingdom. It was selected by the Northern Command as a centre for training Officers for recruiting work. When the work of recruiting was taken over by the Ministry of National Service, the Hull Office was selected as a Provincial centre for training officers for the Ministry.[11]

Those long uneven lines
Standing as patiently
As if they were stretched outside
The Oval or Villa Park,
The crowns of hats, the sun
On moustached archaic faces
Grinning as if it were all
An August Bank Holiday Lark.

Philip Larkin, 'MCMXIV'

Hull recruitment tram. (Courtesy of Hull Museums)

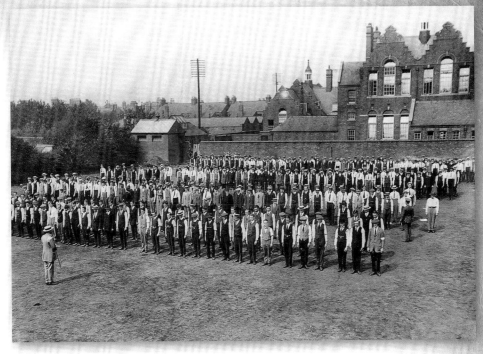

Hull men training at Wenlock Barracks. (From J.A. Tholander scrapbook, courtesy of Hull Museums)

Uniforms were not the only shortage for the tremendous surge of new recruits – weapons were also scarce and training had to be carried out with the use of broomsticks instead of rifles! Uniforms, boots and 400 long-range rifles arrived in November and the men proudly donned their khaki.

Recruitment marches became a regular occurrence through the town and surrounding area and even through Goole, from where a number of Pals had been enlisted. Lincolnshire made its own history with the Pals format; of the hundreds of Pals battalions formed in the country, they were the only one to coin the phrase *Chums* instead of Pals, forming their battalion from former pupils of Winteringham Secondary School, Grimsby. Before their khaki arrived, they were bedecked with surplus Post Office uniforms.

The Commercials were the first service battalion to be raised in Hull as part of Lord Kitchener's New Army, under the Pals scheme, whereby men would serve with their friends. This new battalion, known as the 7th Battalion of the East Yorkshire Regiment, was to

By February 1915, 20,000 men from Hull had volunteered for active service – by the end of the war over 70,000 had served, from a population of just under 300,000.

be 1,000 men strong, made up of clerks and other commercial businessmen, recruiting commencing at Wenlock Barracks, Anlaby Road on 1 September 1914.

Thomas Sheppard believed this Commercials Battalion 'was one of the most successful raised in the country. Largely composed of intelligent and able men, it was soon found to contain a large number of men admirably suited to hold commissions in His Majesty's Forces.'[12] As so many new battalions were formed, the need for commissioned and non-commissioned officers was just as great as the need for privates. Many of the Hull Commercials were promoted to these ranks.

The idea that men would feel more inclined to sign up if they knew they would be serving alongside their friends seemed a stroke of genius but it was to have some horrific consequences. It certainly did encourage recruitment and it was a great comfort to many to be amongst their friends once immersed in the horrors of war, but at the same time it was their friends and colleagues that they saw mutilated and killed before their eyes and, when it was all over and done with, gaping holes were found within companies and streets alike, where pals had joined up, and been killed, together. Communities were torn apart.

A group of eight North East Railway Dock superintendents joined up together on the 7th but by their own admission, 'we are afraid we hardly realised on that beautiful summer's day the strenuous nature of the life we had laid down our pens to embark upon.'[13]

Still, at the beginning, the adventure of war was all the more appealing when accompanied by friends, so a second, then a third and even a fourth Hull Pals Battalion was formed. The second was known as the Tradesmen's Battalion, fulfilling its quota of 1,000 men within three days. B.S. Barnes quotes welder Robert Harris Weasenham, from East Hull, who joined this unit '… to save little Belgium and France.'[14]

The third was the Sportsmen, whose recruitment meeting saw the Honourable F.S. Jackson, famous Yorkshire cricketer and sportsman, give a stirring speech:

The Humberside area supplied over 880 vessels and 9,000 men from the fishing trade. In total 670 vessels were lost from our region, 214 being minesweepers and when a minesweeper went down, nearly half the crew were lost with it.

If there is anyone in this country who feels he should kick something, all I can say is let him go to the front; he will have plenty of opportunities of kicking something there. Let him go forward and kick the backsides of some of those dirty blackguards who have been pillaging, butchering, and sacking all those weak and helpless people in Belgium.[15]

These three battalions had sufficient numbers of men yet there were still plenty coming forward to volunteer so Hull raised a fourth Pals battalion, T'Others, as well as a local reserve battalion, the Bantams. Four Pals battalions was an amazing achievement for a city the size of Hull.

Of course, being a major port, many of Hull's men were used by the Royal and Merchant Navies and there were also other battalions within the East Riding which took our men, including two Territorial battalions, a Yeomanry regiment, a Royal Garrison Artillery Battery, a Field Ambulance of the RAMC and a Field Company of the Royal Engineers. The Divisional Ammunition Column was largely made up of recruits from the city's police force and tramways. At the outbreak, the 4th and 5th Cyclist Battalions of the East Yorkshire Regiment were sent to the coast in preparation for an invasion, digging trenches along the cliff tops in readiness for defence.

Recruitment propaganda card. (Courtesy of Hull Museums)

With such an absence of menfolk, the country relied heavily on women. Women volunteered to help with any aspect they could, from the hundred schoolmistresses who flocked to the City Hall to help with recruitment, to the girls who took on men's roles in the factories, fields, policing and even on the trams. Many of the factories changed their normal production over to production of war articles and the women were given the opportunity to show that they could do 'men's jobs', for the first time in history.

There were also a number of clubs set up to support women while their men were away, such as the social club on Mason Street. An article in the *Eastern Morning News*, dated 14 February 1916, explained that the club had been set up to:

> ... cheer, strengthen and sustain the lives of those whose husbands were on active service, engaged in the highest of all service – the protection of our homes and country from armed invasion and cruel wrong. The club was inaugurated shortly after the outbreak of war by women for women – the wives of soldiers and sailors and their children – in the hope of enabling the womenfolk by the encouragement and assistance afforded them to bear more bravely their burden in the war.

There was a tremendous amount of pressure on men to join up and fight for King and Country. Kitchener's famous pointing picture, 'Your Country Needs You', had an unprecedented effect on the young men of Britain. An overwhelming urge to preserve the spirit of freedom and sovereignty of our country was fostered and to lay down one's life to protect those things held dear, even in so far as lying about one's age. Private John Cunningham was one such 16 year old who in the first queue gave his true age but then, being rejected, joined another queue and stated that he was 18. He was accepted into the Sportsmen's Battalion, no further questions asked.

This excerpt from a letter in the *Hull Daily Mail* on 29 August 1914 illustrates the general feeling people held about the war and recruitment:

We had a perfect right to go to war, and we should have been the veriest skunks and cowards had we kept out of war. That is the honest … opinion of the 'man in the street', and every man with an ounce of English honour and integrity in him is determined to hold up the Government with both hands, and is calmly steeling himself to make whatever sacrifices he can to assist 'K of K' to see this thing through.

SCARBOROUGH LIGHTHOUSE.
AFTER THE GERMAN BOMBARDMENT.

Scarborough lighthouse after the German bombardment. (Courtesy of Hull Museums)

Other posters dominated the social scene so the patriotic call was impossible to ignore. The Union Flag's colours flared out everywhere, *Fight for it, Work for it*. The atrocities the Germans inflicted on the people they invaded was proclaimed to the people, *Remember Belgium, Enlist Today!* Scenes of destruction, women and children in dire peril, *Men of Britain, will you stand this?*

The government even capitalised on the tragic bombing of Scarborough and Whitby in December 1914. Such a wave of outrage and fear was provoked over these civilian deaths, on British soil, that recruitment increased. Soon ceramic souvenirs of the bombed Scarborough lighthouse and medals commemorating the attack were issued, to remind people of the German atrocities and what they were fighting for, ensuring volunteers kept coming forward.

Pressure came from all sides; from friends, work colleagues, neighbours and it was felt a true badge of honour to sign up. Shirley Hills illustrates this patriotic fever demonstrably in a poem she sent to the *Hull Daily Mail* on 26 August 1914:

> *Up! Up! you men, single men of Hull,*
> *Hark your country's call;*
> *Your country has urgent need of you –*
> *Immediate need for all.*
> *To your shame never let it be said*
> *You waited for press-gang's force;*
> *You know the old adage truly says,*
> *'There's nowt like a willing horse.'*

> *Here is just the chance to show your grit –*
> *Loose sweetheart's clinging arms;*
> *If single, able-bodied and fit,*
> *Sooth mother's fond alarms.*
> *Give ready your service and volunteer,*
> *We'll send you off with a ringing cheer;*
> *Better a Hero in battlefield dead,*
> *Than a smug Live Coward safe in bed.*

Percy Cawkwell, known as Corky, joined the RAMC as a stretcher-bearer in 1915. He had previously been rejected from the forces on account of a defect in his eyesight but after a humiliating encounter on a Hull tram in August 1915, he was determined to be taken. He explained in his diary that it was a rare sight by that time to be seen out of uniform and his tram was travelling down Beverley Road when a young woman approached him. 'Why aren't you in uniform, you slacker,' the girl apparently demanded of him. 'Are you afraid to fight?'

Corky says he was both hurt and angry, as he had tried to join up on two previous occasions and after the girl had left him speechless he jumped off the tram in town and made straight for the City Hall. There he bumped into someone he knew who told him the RAMC were taking anybody on, so Corky headed in and joined up on the spot. He was told to come back on Monday morning and that was that.

Corky's experience with the young lass was not an uncommon one at this time. The towns and cities around the country were pasted with propaganda posters and the gossip in the streets was impossible to escape. Everyone knew everyone else and you were looked upon with shame if you had a son out of uniform. There was a common occurrence of girls sending young men envelopes containing a white chicken feather, in an attempt to

Recruitment propaganda card. (Courtesy of Hull Museums)

47

disgrace them, embarrass them and ultimately make them sign up. There was a rush of posters aimed at wives, girlfriends, mothers and women in general, arguing that they should be ashamed if their 'best boy' was not wearing khaki. 'If he does not think that you and your country are worth fighting for – do you think he is worthy of you?'

Where will you look, sonny, where will you look
When your children yet to be
Clamour to learn of the part you took
In the War that kept men free?[16]

Fake telegram used for recruitment and propaganda. (Courtesy of Hull Museums)

Other tactics were employed, such as the fake telegrams sent to mothers, bearing messages such as 'Mothers do not allow the finger of scorn to be directed towards your husband or sons. Send them to protect you and yours now'. Signed 'Tommy Atkins'. Or those addressed to 'N.O.T. Yetter' asking 'is it fair to expect me to fight for both of us any longer you will have to do your little bit.' Again signed 'Tommy Atkins'. For 'I.N. Different, Belgium Scarborough Lusitania Zeppelin Raids E13 and more to follow unless you do your duty now.'

The government also created and issued special badges for those men who were helping the war effort in ways other than being a soldier. This meant that they could show their badge or certificate when they were confronted by people demanding to know why they had not joined up.

Even factories and firms were encouraging their workers to enlist, as this letter in *The Snapper* from a Beverley firm, Messrs Richard Hodgson and Sons, illustrates:

> We understand that the Government have now to some extent filled their orders for equipment and are no longer in urgent want for leather for this purpose. Under these circumstances, and seeing the great need for recruits, we feel sure there are some men in these works who would now be of greater service in the Army, and on hearing from any desirous of joining, we will make every effort to fill their places by men of non-military age until their return.[17]

All this coupled with the promise of adventure and glory, of going somewhere new, saw line after line of new recruits sign up – and, after all, it was common knowledge that the war would be over in six months!

The atmosphere in the city was one of tremendous morale, the feeling of joining together, of doing your bit. The young men were joining all the other young men of the whole country in order to defend their homeland. The thought of being killed never entered most lads' minds and the idea of killing the enemy sounded grand. By the time the realisation hit that they might not return home, it was too late. For many, it was to be the first time they saw their pal killed beside them that reality finally hit home.

Corky described leaving Paragon Station that Monday morning, with dozens of people waving off their loved ones, knowing it would be some time before they would see each other again. Once at the barracks the soldiers were issued with uniforms, with which some were overjoyed, as they had never had any underwear before! 'They were the ones I noticed at breakfast having second helpings.'[18] One soldier told Corky that this was the first time in his life that he had eaten three meals a day.

It was all a great adventure at the start. 'If this war has done nothing else, it has given renewed health and strength to many. It has even taken thousands of men of the street loafer or 'corner boy' type and made them into fine, healthy specimens of humanity.'[19]

Soon enough, though, the men learned the brutal reality of war. As Gerald Dennis, a Hull volunteer in the 21st King's Royal Rifle Corps, said, the true nature of why they had joined up was lost to the men, once they were surrounded by death, blood, mud and fear. 'We're here because we're here because …'[20]

Needlers factory had fifty-five of its men apply for enlistment. Fourteen were enlisted under Lord Derby's scheme and eleven had been rejected. As it employed largely female labour these figures showed that 75 per cent of their eligible men had offered themselves. Of those not eligible thirteen were performing services as special constables.

The Defence of the Realm Act (DORA) was passed soon after the start of the war, on 8 August 1914, imposing restrictions on citizens in an attempt to maximise security and prevent invasion. The censorship of letters and newspaper articles was a high priority, but there were restrictions on such activities as kite flying (which could attract Zeppelin bombers) or wasting food. The Act also gave the government the powers to requisition any land or buildings it deemed necessary for the war effort. The *Hull Daily Mail* lists examples of farmers asking for compensation for their land being commandeered, articles about food factories being taken over by Food Controllers, news of the use of oil being restricted for heating purposes, restrictions on the sale of agricultural horses, reports about road halts for motor vehicles leaving and entering the city, limitations on alcohol intake and countless other everyday activities which affected the daily lives of the people. It was not just the soldiers and their families who were affected by the war – it was everyone.

'Important to Photographers – The "Mail" is officially informed that no photographs may be taken in Hull without the permission of the competent Military Authority. No photographic apparatus may be carried in any part of Hull without permission.'[21]

On 29 December 1914, a lighting order was reported under DORA: 'The lighting of shop windows, whether exterior or interior, must be reduced to the minimum required for carrying out business, and must be so shaded as to throw no light on the street. Proceedings will be taken against all persons committing a breach of the order.'

A few examples of these breaches were given on 10 August 1915, when Alfred Lee was fined 10*s* 6*d* for failing to obscure a light in his jeweller's shop in Whitefriargate, T. Theakston was fined the same for showing a light in the library, Emmanuel Salton the same for 'showing an incandescent light in a window' and James Silver of Whitefriargate was fined £2 2*s* for a similar offence. Another Hull man was fined this amount, a report on 27 September 1917 stated, for losing his police registration card – a serious offence under the Act.

The *Hull Daily Mail*, in relation to a plea from Bridlington, asked, on 22 December 1914, 'that in view of the Christmas holidays, the military authorities be requested to relax the restrictions on the right of access to the piers, sea walls, cliffs, and foreshore, so that the residents and visitors may be allowed access thereto as usual.'

At the end of 1915 there appeared a statement:

No New Year Buzzers: The Press are requested to draw the attention of owners of factories and workshops of all descriptions who have buzzers that, under the defence of the Realm Act, no buzzers other than those authorised are allowed to be blown. Therefore, the usual signals on the birth of the New Year must not be blown.

Once enforced conscription was introduced in 1916, new clauses were added to DORA, such as mentioned in the *Hull Daily Mail* on 9 February 1918:

> A new Regulation has been added to the Defence of the Realm Act relating to the duties of employers of men of military age. A clause of the Regulation requires that 'before any male person apparently of military age is taken into or engages in any employment in Great Britain or a contract for such employment is entered into with him, the proposed employer shall take all reasonable steps to obtain the production of any certificate of exemption or protection affecting him and other evidence relating to his position for the time being with regard to liability for military service.

Restrictions curbed all normal activities to some extent, countrywide, but certainly initially the public were willing to comply with anything that helped their side to win the war. Sacrifice was borne ever bravely.

3

WORK OF WAR

One of biggest local industrial changes in Hull in the First World War was that of the fishing industry. Hull has a long history of merchants, trading and fishing and was the third largest port in England at that time. As early as 1907 the Admiralty saw the potential of the fishing trawlers and their crews as minesweepers, should war occur. At the outbreak of war, Germany began laying mines in the North Sea to prevent food supplies reaching Britain. The Admiralty requisitioned the trawlers, the vessels becoming minesweepers, being refitted and redeployed and many fishermen of Hull and Grimsby were utilised for their skills. The Humberside area supplied over 880 vessels, 300 of which were Hull fishing trawlers, plus 9,000 men from the fishing trade. Over 800 Hull merchant seamen lost their lives through enemy action in the war and the Wilson Line, Hull's largest merchant shipping company, lost over forty vessels out of eighty-four, and around 300 crew members.

John Markham[22] quotes a local man, Alfred Dee, who had one brother in the navy on the minesweepers and another on grain runs from America to England. Both were very dangerous yet vital jobs and by 1917 the Germans were sinking one ship in every three. Alfred said he remembered leaving school in 1917 and 'going down to the King George Dock to meet my brother. There was a coloured cook on the ship and I asked him

On 18 December 1914 a fleet of Grimsby trawlers was ordered to clear a field of a hundred mines off Cayton Bay. By the following April sixty-nine mines had been cleared but fourteen steamships, four minesweepers and two patrol vessels had been lost.

if there was any chance of a job on board. He said they could do with a cabin boy. So I told my brother and he said, "You're not coming on this ship. If she gets hit there'll be two gone from the family."'

Hull's industry played an important part in the war, aside from the trawlers and minesweepers. We had numerous factories within the city that, at the outbreak of war, made a huge contribution, changing their normal production over to 'articles of war'. Even Needlers sweet factory, founded in 1902, began placing adverts which stated the soldiers at the front found their Military Mints and other sweets, 'a solace for all wars'.

When war broke out Needlers had been obtaining all their bottles from Germany and as they used 5,000 bottles a week it took some time to reorganise themselves. Fortunately English makers came to their assistance.

Gas mask made by Reckitt & Sons. (Courtesy of Hull Museums)

Fenners, a Hull company operating since 1861, manufacturing leather belting goods, relied heavily on exporting before war broke out. Up to 70 per cent of sales were exports, this fell dramatically by over 90 per cent once war commenced. The company survived, however, managing to increase its sales in the UK.

Priestman Brothers was an engineering company based in Hull since the 1870s. After the war the company's tank-mounted crane was used in the rebuilding of French villages and battlefields, which had been destroyed in the conflict.

Reckitt's, as well as sending many men out to the front and making war supplies, created a hospital within the factory:

Factory Hospital at Reckitt's, now used for wounded soldiers. The soldiers are surprised with their luxurious food and with the ease and comfort provided. The nurses have many delightful surprises. Many times on returning from their dinner they find their duties done by the convalescent men. Ward dusted, dishes washed, but never the medicines taken![23]

Mrs McKernon who was interviewed in 1982 remembered Smith and Nephews:

… it was only a small place against the pier. They did the first field dressings in the First World War there. It was 4/6d a week if you were lucky because you had to do 100 for 6d. The trays used to come in and there would be a khaki bandage, a piece of lint, a little bandage with a little piece of lint inside, a piece of gauze, a bandage and a safety pin. They used to come wrapped up from the machines below – in a sort of waterproof wrapping. Then you put them in a tray. It took you all day to get 6d, so at the end of the week you didn't always get 4/6d. You might get 4 shillings because some were quicker than others.[24]

Every Tommy in the war was issued with these field dressings, which were kept in a little pocket on the inside of his tunic.

Joseph Rank Ltd of Clarence Street was founded in 1875, a flour millers, corn merchant and seed crusher. During the war years the company employed 3,000 workers, many of whom were women, and Joseph Rank himself was asked to become a member of the Wheat Control Board, as food supplies were a major problem.

Hull, like many cities, turned its attention to munitions-making, at factories such as Rose Downs and Thompsons. Previously manufacturers of general engineering equipment, they changed to shell production for the sake of the war, employing many women for this essential work.

Another change for the town was that many German shops were closed down, due to the hostile feelings the people at home harboured towards them.

Every aspect of life was affected by the war. The *Hull Times* showed how Hull's allotments were being utilised for the sake of the war.[25] The trams and railways were given priority for war business. Buildings were commandeered for recruiting, the wounded, soldiers' rest places and even social clubs, as shown in *The Snapper*:

In the Autumn of 1914, when it was found that Hull was to become a garrison town again and thousands of men of all branches of the Army were being accommodated ... the pressing need for a good sized building for the use of the troops as a club was at once manifest. Various influential people got together and in conjunction with the G.O.C. Humber Defences, approached the Hull Corporation and obtained the hire of Beverley Road Baths.[26]

This Soldier's Club had a library, entertainment in the shape of weekly concerts, sing-songs, plays etc., a rifle range, refreshments bar, billiards and other games, a reading room, letter-writing facilities, band performances and even electric light! So popular and well known was this club that the local newspapers had soldiers writing in about it from all over the country. Private Galwey of the Lancashire Fusiliers wrote that:

... the Soldier's Club on Beverley Road is so well known and appreciated by its frequenters – the soldiers themselves – that it would be superfluous for me to try to make it better known, were it not that soldiers come and soldiers go. But I often wonder, do the good citizens of Hull, who organise this club for Tommy, know what a vast amount of good it has done ... if there is one thing that is valued, more than another it is the great facilities to the soldiers for writing. At present a hundred men can sit down in comfort to write their letters, and the quantity of writing paper used shows at once how much it is sought after. Between 8,000 and 12,000 envelopes are used in a week ... we wish to thank the citizens of Hull for the kindness that has always been shown to us.

Along with this there were other venues that catered for soldiers and their families, such as the Soldier's and Sailor's Wives Club in Mason Street and various voluntary aid attachments.

The work of Hull's Peel House during the war was of upmost importance.[27] It was the headquarters of the Voluntary Aid Detachments of Hull and East Riding and they organised the first three hospitals to be started in Hull: the Royal Naval Hospital, staffed by VAD nurses; Lady Sykes' Hospital, situated in the Metropole Hall and later transferred to France; and the Reckitt's Hospital, also staffed by VAD nurses. The Saint John Voluntary Aid Detachment Hospital based at the Newland Girls' School on Cottingham Road was also pivotal, as was the Rest Station in Paragon Station. Hundreds of troops passed through this station and the rest canteen was greatly welcomed. There were also a number of other Rest Stations situated throughout the city staffed by volunteers, to aid those wounded by the raids. There was also an officers' hospital, Brooklands, on Cottingham Road, which catered for sick officers connected with the Humber Garrison. One soldier treated here was J.R.R. Tolkien, who spent eighteen months there suffering from trench fever.

Hull's Prisoner of War Fund sent out over 130,000 parcels to British soldiers being held in Germany, parcels which were often lifesavers.

Reckitt's

The world-famous Hull firm, Reckitt's, was hugely influential during the war. Immediate to the outbreak, seventy employees were called up, this figure rising to 820 by 1917. The company converted their social hall into a military hospital, the Reckitt's VAD Hospital, approved by the military authority in November 1914, the first patients arriving in the December.

With forty-five beds, in the four years three months it was open, 2,910 patients were treated here and, by all accounts, it was the favourite place to convalesce.

Colonel Tatham from the Humber Garrison Medical Service wrote a tribute to the hospital and staff, quoted by B.S. Barnes in *Known to the Night*, p.13:

> ... the patients who have been there greatly appreciate the care and kindness bestowed upon them. Many of them have told me they were so well looked after and received so many little extras and kindnesses that Reckitt's was the hospital that men wished to get into if they could.

The company also billeted troops on their premises and Sir James Reckitt promptly offered to house a large number of Belgian refugees in October 1914. Being a Quaker himself, Sir James Reckitt was opposed to war but when the inevitable occurred he did all he could for his people, as he did in peacetime.

Cecil Slack, on becoming a prisoner of war in 1918, was 'adopted' by the firm as one to whom the company would send out parcels, for which Slack was infinitely grateful.

At the end of the war, after a total of 1,108 people from their worldwide workforce had become members of the forces and 153 employees had lost their lives, with nearly a further 50 per cent of the remainder wounded or disabled, a memorial fountain was erected in the grounds of Reckitt's, depicting *Sacrifice* with a dead youth at her feet, brandishing a torch and representing that bequeathed by everyone, for King and Country.

The Reckitt's memorial fountain, with thanks to Reckitt Benckiser for allowing me to take the photograph.

Peel House organised and sent out numerous packages to the East Yorkshire lads at the front. They were designed to make life more bearable, with food parcels for prisoners of war and special Christmas Comforts. The Freehold Bread Fund, from Freehold Street, also raised a substantial amount of money to provide bread for these prisoners.

These parcels meant such a lot to the men, as Hull man Cecil Slack stated emphatically to his sweetheart Doris when he was taken prisoner of war. When bread arrived, although mouldy and hard from delays, he wrote that it was a significantly important day in his life, to have food again, to eat, to stay alive. He said he would remember that day ever after, which he did, making a donation to Oxfam every year.

Alice Markham's older brother George had been taken a prisoner and interred in Germany for nine months. The strict censoring made his letters home very sparse but after the war they found out he had been at Ypres and was wounded when the Germans shelled their village. He was taken prisoner and described the food at the POW camp as very poor. 'They were given hard, dark bread and he brought a piece home at the end of the war to show us. There was also a lot of spinach and watery soup.'[28]

Military hospital in Hull. (Courtesy of Hull Museums)

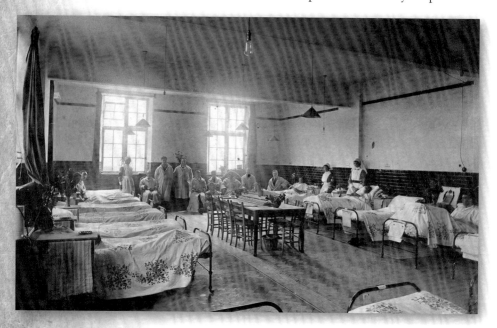

VAD hospital, Cottingham Road, Hull. (Courtesy of Hull Museums)

Many fishermen and merchant seamen were captured in the North Sea and interned at detention camps, such as Ruhleben. As food was scarce for everyone in wartime the prisoners were poorly fed, so food parcels sent out were lifesavers. Hull's Prisoner of War Fund sent out over 130,000 parcels and the Hull Seamen's Union also sent parcels out as well as providing money, clothing and coal for those in need at home.

B.S. Barnes quotes from Peter McNally, a Hull Pals recruit in 1914, who became a prisoner of war when trying to resist the German offensive in May 1918.[29] He was taken to Giessen POW Camp in Germany. He stated that on the journey there the food was terrible, when they got any, and every man was expected to work for his scanty share. The treatment at the hands of the Germans was brutal, with severe daily beatings being meted out and anything to quash morale.

Britain was very reliant on imported food and supplies, a fact that the Germans exploited during the war by using U-boats to sink our merchant ships. Even though ration cards were not issued until 1918, people were implored not to waste food, to save and recycle where they could, not just for their own sakes, but for the lives of the sailors bringing it home. The *Hull*

61

Daily Mail ran an advert from Maypole Dairy on 1 January 1918 apologising for its queues for margarine. It explained, however, that they would rather ration out their supplies to give everyone a chance of obtaining some, than merely selling the whole week's output in one day. 'It is better for a poor woman to have a chance of getting supplies from a queue then to get no supplies of an essential food like Margarine.'

Mrs Maclean was interviewed in 1980 about her time in Hull during the war:

> It was very difficult to get food in the first war. My mother used to go to one shop and I would go to another and my sister would go to another. Everybody had to do that, it was terrible. They had a job to get stuff into the shops, I think. The thing that was most short was butter. You could only get a bit of butter. I used to go along to the shop and my sister would be two or three behind me and we'd get two or three potatoes each. My mother went to the butcher's, and perhaps if we went to another one we might get something. We used to get bits and pieces all over.[30]

Emma Keeitch talked about her time working for the Hull brewery firm Moore and Robson's in Raywell Street. She explained how all the young drivers had left the brewery for the army at the start of the war, so drivers were in short supply:

> By about 1915 beer itself was in short supply, so the brewery only delivered to their own houses. Any private pub or club had to come to the brewery to collect their orders. I've seen them come with handcarts, cars, all sorts lined up down Raywell Street waiting to be served. But they could only have four boxes at a time, each one holding two dozen bottles, and I've had many a sovereign offered me if only I would let them have another box. But I wouldn't have taken their money and I couldn't possibly have done it anyway.[31]

When the Parliamentary recruiting circular was distributed in the North, thousands of women, as the country's new workforce, a large proportion of whom belonged to the leisured and middle classes, offered their services to the nation. It was stated that 'women have shown remarkable aptitude for picking up the work', in the manufacture of shells and other explosives.[32]

Propaganda had its part to play in encouraging women to do their bit, just as the men were, and the Ministry of Munitions, the Women's Land Army and the Queen Mary's Army Auxiliary Corps all offered women positions previously reserved for men. The National Union of Women Workers organised voluntary patrols in Hull, acting as a morality police force.[33] Other work ranged from seed crushing and paint manu-

Studio portrait of a woman in a VAD uniform. (Courtesy of Hull Museums)

facture to transport and heavy industry. The *Hull Daily Mail* often ran articles on women's work for the war effort, as they 'were being trained in ship building, the dock yard, transport and munitions', as well as growing food, postal work, telegraph messengers, even taxi driving! 'The woman taxi-driver is being introduced at Hull. One proprietor, however, expressed the opinion that he does not think that driving at night is suitable for women, especially if they have to go on to the docks.'[34]

Alice Markham, whose family had a farm in Holderness, remembers that when the war started all the younger men on the farm left to join the army, including her brother George. She mentions that some soldiers were sent to work on the farm as the fit men had all left, but these were not country men, and they were not used to such work:

Women munitions workers. (Courtesy of Hull Museums)

We had a butcher, a bank clerk and a greengrocer and one who was almost blind, and I have to admit it was rather amusing to see how they all worked. Later the farmer's two daughters and myself had to help during harvest and other busy times. We bought ourselves a land army outfit of breeches, shirt, coat, hat and the usual puttees for our legs. We were always praised for our work as we had been brought up to farm life and could use a fork or any other tool better than the soldiers.

Government officials came to the farm to inspect all the horses as they needed them to pull the heavy guns that were used in France at that time. They only wanted the very best and chose some of our favourites.

As we were on the east coast we were now in a very important part of the country. One result was that there seemed more life for us all. Concerts and dances were held in the villages, I suppose the idea being to keep everyone as happy as possible even though there was a war on.[35]

Munitions work was a huge source of employment for women such as the production of shells at Rose Downs and Thompson. The work was hard with long hours and the Grimsby shell factory made 6in shells, which were nearly too heavy for the women to manage.

John Markham interviewed Alfred Dee who used to work at the big Hull and Barnsley Wagon Works on Springhead Road:

I hadn't been there long before they started women on painting the wagons. It was the first time women had been doing work like that. Some of them were even doing heavy work because this would be about 1918 and so many men had gone into the war and been killed that they had to take women. It had to be like that and we didn't think anything about it.

He also mentions an interview with Carrie Dawson, who used to work at Hopper's in Barton, on munitions, drilling holes in the noses of shells. 'We wore a cap to put your hair under. We had tunics with belts. It was the first time I'd ever worn trousers.'

Annie Ralph told how she got a job with British Oil and Cake Mill in Wincolmlee when her husband signed up, as she was very poor, with two children to keep:

We used to work from six in the morning till five at night and we got good wages. I really furnished my home from what I earned. It was heavy work, barrowing and loading lorries, but the atmosphere was friendly … though one man was hostile towards us women. But we were not taking men's work. We were doing men's work to help the war effort.

Eva Riggs was 14 in 1914 and lived just across the Humber in Lincolnshire. By the time she was 17 she had seen many women take over men's work, as more and more young men left to join the war:

I watched the conductresses on the trams and kept thinking I would love to be a conductress. I went and had an interview. I filled a form in and I put that my age was seventeen. However, when the chap came to look at my form he said, 'You have to be twenty one!' 'Oh,' I said, 'I did want to try. It would be helping the war.' I went on and on. In the end he agreed to make a false entry and put twenty one. So I was on the trams till the war was

Celebrations in a Hull military hospital. (Courtesy of Hull Museums)

over. I loved it. We used to get up at four early turn and I've taken a load of miners on my tram – as many as could get to the pit for the five o'clock shift. We had a day off each week. We worked Saturday and Sunday so that was six days, but if somebody didn't turn up for an afternoon shift and you'd just gone into the depot to take your tickets in, they'd say, 'We want you to do this afternoon's shift. So and so hasn't turned up.' If you did a double shift that earned you a lot of money. I worked from five o'clock till eleven at night many a time during the war. As soon as I got in I used to fall asleep.

Food was scarce but those that were in uniform who were doing their bit were allowed to go in first if there was a queue. There used to be queues just for two ounces of butter, one egg, a bit of cheese or two ounces of bacon.

With 2,128 allotment holders in Hull, over 280 acres were cultivated for the war effort. Hull had over 150 schoolboys under instruction on the allotments. Some 600–700 East Yorkshire women registered for work on the land. In total 982 did some form of work, on farms, allotments or market gardens.

Audrey Waters was 15 the year the war started. She remembered Newland High School on Cottingham Road, which had just been newly completed, was taken over and used as a hospital:

> As a young girl, I used to be taken there to sing to the troops, poor beggars. A captive audience if ever there was. My mother was very good hearted and she used to say that they did not want pretty girls in the kitchen; they wanted them where they could see them. She herself was a voluntary helper in the kitchen and she kept a bag of white flour and she used to bake batches of teacakes and send me down to the hospital with them to give them to old soldiers who had nobody to visit them. There were a lot of V.A.D.s and some professional nurses. The V.A.Ds had a grey uniform and starched white apron down to their ankles and black stockings.[36]

Woman in nurse's uniform. (Courtesy of Hull Museums)

Destiny: War Letters of Captain Jack Oughtred contains many letters from Jack, fighting at the front, to his sweetheart, Phyllis, left at home in Hull. Through their long-distance courtship, spanning three and some years, we gain an intimate insight into both what Jack was seeing and experiencing on the front and what Phyllis and the people of Hull were going through at home. Phyllis was a VAD nurse in the Argyle Street Naval Hospital where she worked long hours as well as having the added pressure of a journey from Swanland and back every day. Before joining the East Yorkshire Battalion, Jack worked for the London Joint Stock Bank in Hull. One letter, dated 9 February 1915, informs Phyllis that he has asked for leave from his job, in order to join up, but states, 'I hear that girls are going to be installed in the Bank to fill up the vacant

Rose, Downs and Thompsons' munitions factory employed three females in July 1914 but by October 1918 this figure had risen to 359, 13 under 18 years of age and 346 between 18 and 51 years old.

places until the end of the war. Some rather curious times in store for those remaining, don't you think.'[37] This clearly shows that previously such work had not been considered fit for women. Nevertheless their help was essential early on in the war.

In the diary that Hull lad Percy Cawkwell kept during the war, we read that he got some leave before going off to France for the first time and on the journey home he started chatting to some lads from the Yorks and Lancs regiments. Two girls joined in the conversation, '[they] told us they were on munitions in Leeds "we make the bullets you shoot" they both said proudly.' Corky was surprised by this; 'I thought about how much this war was changing things. I couldn't remember a time before the war when two young girls would have joined the conversation of two young men they didn't know, and they had been on a short holiday together by themselves in Blackpool.'[38]

Mention should be made of Hull's first woman GP, Dr Mary Murdoch, who, incidentally, was also the first woman to drive herself in the streets of Hull, in her De Dion car. She had first worked at the Victoria Hospital for Sick Children, in Park Street,

Hull military hospital. (Courtesy of Hull Museums)

in 1893, becoming Hull's first GP in 1910. She was a pioneer in Hull's Suffragette Movement, as well as working tirelessly for the sick and wounded. Unfortunately she fell ill with a severe cold and died in 1916, but she was fondly remembered by all Hull citizens. In 1914 she had pledged to raise £250 to reopen the babies ward at the Victoria Hospital and immediately after her death £962 was subscribed to redeem this pledge and endow a cot in her name. Mentioning this memorial, the *Hull Daily Mail* stated that 'perhaps in the times still far distant this memorial may be an incitement even for some who did not know her to emulate her courage and her devotion to duty'.[39]

Edith Cavell, the nurse executed in Belgium by the Germans, had a sister who was a nurse in a hospital at Withernsea. Florence Cavell was the first matron there.

The Hull District War Refugees Committee for Belgian Refugees was set up on 7 September 1914 with its headquarters at Bowlalley Lane, Hull. Of its 500 volunteer helpers, 400 were women, aiding over 1,200 refugees in total.

One thing that can be said about this terrible and tragic war was that it drew people together, class divisions were broken down, the poor and rich alike gave their time and services to those who needed it. Food was scarce for everyone, roles changed, fear presided and everyone lost someone they loved.

4

NEWS FROM THE FRONT

From the Trenches
Now Private A. and Private B.
Were much more brave than you or me,
For as one night we shivered with fright
While the German star-shells burn ghastly bright,
And the 'Johnsons' burst with a sickening roar,
Bang in the middle of our trench board floor,
And the shrapnel whizzed and seemed to say
'It's a 'Bhility Wallah' you will get today'
And nearer still to the stars so bright,
The 'heavies' tore through that awful night
With a noise like a crane or a railway train
Till all of us shivered once again!
But Private A. and Private B.
Didn't care a damn for this Hell you see,
For they were busy — mashing tea!!

C.L. 07.07.1915[40]

Feet deep in mud, soldiers fought, ate, slept, washed and defecated in narrow trenches, open to the elements with the smell of dead men and putrefaction as constant companions. Enormous rats and blood-sucking lice were inevitable, causing diseases such as trench fever, which infected around 800,000 Allied soldiers.

Just heard today from an old schoolpal just home wounded from the front. He says it looks hopeless out there and is absolutely 'Hell on earth'. I often wonder whether one will come through this business.[41]

The conditions of trench warfare in the First World War are as unimaginable to us now as is life in another hundred years time. It was a war like no other. The incessant threat of imminent death was a constant, with heavy explosions all around, alive with flying shrapnel and friends shot by snipers before one's very eyes. The deep mud, the inescapable cold, the monster rats feeding off the rotting dead, the smell, the lice, the trench foot, the fatigue, hunger, brutality and fear. It is a wonder anyone could survive it for a day, let alone four years. 'Trenches were like the Old Harbour at Hull – if you did not want to be drowned or up to your neck in mud, you had to walk on top.'[42]

Corky also describes how bad the trench conditions were. Two days of persistent rain and the trenches were feet deep in water and mud. June 1916:

We discovered the sometimes impossibly hard work of retrieving wounded on stretchers while wading in thigh deep mud and water … trying to do my work under intense artillery bombardment … How many times I threw myself down, pulling my comrades down with me into the slimy mud, with the wounded man as well, to the bottom of the trench.[43]

Margaret Hardcastle's great-uncle always managed to convey a sense of humour in his letters home, such as this one from 14 July 1916:

Are you at Hornsea now? Tell Babs when she is digging on the sands that 'uncle' digs himself holes in the ground to live in but it is not so nice as digging sand castles and much harder work. Hope the holiday will do you all good. Wish I could have a few days off. Am living in hopes of a finish before so very long.

Then there were the bloody battles, where Pals and comrades fell one after another and it was kill or be killed, even if that meant having to bayonet a 16-year-old lad.

The Pals depended upon each other in the trenches, for loyalty, friendship and camaraderie. They needed the morale boost in such dire conditions, but the downside was the heartbreak of seeing close friends die. 'I awoke feeling miserable and dissatisfied, for is not today a Bank Holiday? No holiday for us though. Every day is like its predecessor and very often worse!' [44]

Hull men serving with the Territorials of the 4th Battalion saw their first action at Ypres in 1915, the Battle of St Julien, and they fought at the Somme in 1916 and 1918. They took heavy losses at Arras and Passchendaele in 1917, then again in Lys, just to mention a few.

Andrew Winfield's great-grandfather, Percival Charles Markham, was a lance corporal in the 1st Battalion of the Lincolnshire Reserves. Born in Caistor in 1886 he moved to Hull and became a policeman at Priory Road Police Station, marrying Annie Fratson in 1907. He died in September 1914 during the Battle of Aisne, although at the time he was listed as missing in action. This was one of the most significant battles in the whole of the war, as it marked the beginning of trench warfare. A newspaper cutting from the time reports that Percival was seen running out of a trench and falling due to a wound in his leg but what happened to him after this is unknown. The newspaper cutting, which Andrew had kept, stated:

[Percival Charles Markham was in the] 1st Lincolns, and a member of the Hull Police Force, having for seven years been stationed at Gordon-street Police Station. Mrs Markham ... received the last news in the form of a letter from her husband on September 16th, the letter being dated Sept. 10th. Mrs Markham is naturally very anxious to hear some news of her husband. She has written to or personally interrogated about 20 soldiers belonging to the 1st Lincolns, who have been home for various causes. Yesterday morning she received the

Lance Corporal Percival Charles Markham was a reservist before the war started. (Courtesy of Andrew Winfield)

following letter ... 'In reply to your letter, I am very sorry you have not heard what has become of Mr Markham yet. I was in hopes you had heard something before now. As you know, Mr Markham and I were old pals, therefore I also have been anxious about him. But I am afraid we shall be some time before we shall hear anything about him, and I am sorry I cannot tell you much, but it was at the battle of the Aisne of Sept 14th, we were very hard pressed and had to retire. We got scattered about a great deal, so, of course, we did not know much about each other, and it was at this time he was missing.

For a while people believed he may have been taken prisoner, but as time went on it became clear he was one of the fallen.

The Aisne (1914–15)
We first saw fire on the tragic slopes
Where the flood-tide of France's early gain,
Big with wrecked promise and abandoned hopes,
Broke in a surf of blood along the Aisne

The charge her heroes left us, we assumed,
What, dying, they reconquered, we preserved,
In the chill trenches, harried, shelled, entombed,
Winter came down on us, but no man swerved.

Alan Seeger

The Hull Pals were posted to Egypt in December 1915 to defend the Suez Canal from Turkish attack. They spent Christmas in Egypt and the men found it very strange being somewhere hot for that season. When they were finally moved to France in 1916 the marked contrast in the weather was extreme, much of France being covered in snow.

The Hull Pals were present at the infamous slaughter at the Somme, where men became 'just like falling stalks of corn'. One Private Aust forever afterwards remembered the cries coming from no-man's-land. 'I have always been haunted by the voice of one man, obviously delirious, who kept crying "Mother, mother!"'[45]

Hull Pal John Cunningham's valiant bravery during the Battle of the Ancre, the final offensive of the Somme, earned him the Victoria Cross. He was a private in the 12th Battalion of the East Yorkshire Regiment and, as the *London Gazette* later recorded, he:

> ... proceeded with a bombing section up a communication trench. Much opposition was encountered and the rest of the section became casualties. Collecting all the bombs from the casualties, this gallant soldier went on alone. Having expended all his bombs, he then returned for a fresh supply and again proceeded to the communication trench, where he met a party of ten of the enemy. These he killed and cleared the trench up to the enemy line. His conduct throughout the day was magnificent.

The Somme took many a Hull man's life. Corky, on stretcher-bearer duties there, described that first day:

> I had seen the wounded already in England ... Here was another world. Nothing had prepared me for the conditions that I and others had to cope with as this great battle began. Here for the next forty-eight hours it was to be a shambles, dead and wounded, cut to pieces, covered in blood, an outdoor butcher's shop. Within half an hour of the battle beginning we were busy. At first walking wounded came out of the line ... But then what had at first been a ragged intermittent line of men became a queue, then a shambling, bleeding, moaning crowd until it was not possible to move in the trenches.
>
> Men lay thickly one against the other. We rapidly began to run out of supplies ... we began searching the dead for wound dressings. There was little we could do now except to continue to carry those with a chance

of survival back to the rear. There we lay them in any space we could find, or if they had already died on the way to 'White City', which happened more times than I care to count, they were unceremoniously tipped on the ground.

As the night fell there was another ordeal to come … the sounds made by the wounded left out in the open … simple cries for help or indications as to where they were or awful screams of pain and muffled pleas to God and Mother to help them.

The next day was much the same:

… wounds were almost exclusively the result of machine-gun bullets, punctured stomachs, smashed legs, shoulders and arms or chest wounds. Slipping and sliding, jolting and bumping into what was left of trench walls, we carried them back. We became sticky with the mixture of mud and blood that covered us. We were so much stained it was difficult to see the original khaki of our uniforms.

On the 5th, after a rough five days at the front and a day out, Corky's MO asked for volunteers to go back over the top to search for wounded:

Every member of the ambulance stepped forward. The sight that greeted us deserved the name of 'Battle Field'. On a battle field you had to watch where you were putting your feet, and this [while] carrying a groaning mature man who couldn't keep still because of his pain. One false step and the most obnoxious stench was released as a distended belly you thought was solid ground, caved in.

All the talk of Kitchener's heroic army of Pals is now just the shattered body of a youth … who a few days ago had everything before him.[46]

Stanley William's[47] elder brother who, like Stan, served with the East Yorkshire Yeomanry, had been severely wounded in the head during the Somme. He lay for days in no-man's-land before being rescued by Canadian troops. He did not return to war and it is said splinters of bone continued to exit through his eye until his death in 1958.

Gerald Dennis was also present at the Somme:

My greatest realisation was that in England I had been taught very little about warfare on the Western Front and … the training did not prepare me for the trench conditions.

Heavy shells continued to sing overhead … although our main aim was to press on, we did look to the right and left occasionally in order to keep in line or keep in touch with our own groups, and on such occasions were sad to see one man stumble head foremost, another blown into the air, another collapse in a heap, one nearby with blood streaming from his face. All this time we had to keep on moving forward and not stop to help.

On an informal sort of parade [after their mission] a roll call was taken. Unshaven and unwashed, dirty and haggard-looking, the tired survivors answered their names. The horrors of the attack had left their marks on some of them. They looked around unbelievingly – where was their platoon? Where the Company? The Company was now only as big as a platoon and the battalion little more than the size of a Company. It was estimated that just over a third of the battalion had returned. Our Division, the 41st and the last of Kitchener's battalions, had lost on that day just over three-quarters of a thousand men.

At the camp I was astonished to see two men crying … our beloved Padre … our popular 'C' Company Sergeant-Major. They just could not believe that the lads … had gone. To live among, work with, look after and share privations with sixty men for nine months and then to find almost two-thirds killed, wounded or missing under such terrible conditions had meant such a lot to them. For special work done on September 15th, the battalion was awarded three Military Crosses and sixteen Military Medals.

Letters were swiftly sent home after roll calls, saying who was wounded/killed/missing. Dennis wrote home saying he was OK, but that 'I am afraid that the worst has happened to Willie (Spence).' As he explained in his diary:

He lived in the same street as I did … mother was in the habit of standing at our front gate many times a week, waiting for the postman to see if there was any news from me. Willie scarcely ever wrote home so his mother also stood at her gate watching to see if the postman called at our house. When she saw that he left a letter she came across and asked for news … we were in the same platoon. That awful morning she came across as usual and mother, not waiting for the usual question, handed her the letter so that she could read for herself.[48]

The Hull Pals suffered heavy losses at the Somme but worse was to come for them in 1917 at Oppy Wood.

May 1917 saw all four Hull Pals battalions stationed at the Battle of Arras with the mission to attack and take the village of Oppy. However, the German defences here were very strong, with thick belts of barbed wire and deadly machine guns stationed amongst the trees, as the Germans were aware of the proposed attack. On the 3rd the attack failed, the heavy fire cutting men down in swathes, and the Hull Pals lost more men in this battle than in any other single action during the war, with over 40 per cent being killed in just a few days and many more injured or missing.

Frank Caborn gave a vivid account of his role in the attack. It was amongst the roar and crash of the cacophony of shells that their captain told them they were going over the top in five minutes:

The four Hull Pals battalions formed the 92nd Brigade which, along with 93rd Brigade, 94th Brigade and the KOYLIs made up the 31st Division – the New Army of Kitchener volunteers from the towns and cities of northern England. On the first day of battle the 31st Division lost 1,900 casualties.

I may forget many things, but I shall never forget the intensity of those words. The gates of Hell seemed open and many a gallant lad offered a silent prayer and gave a fleeting thought of home, and to those who loved them. The next minute we advanced … bullets were dropping round us like rain and bombs were being hurled in every direction.[49]

Frank survived the battle, but was wounded in the hand and back. 'Hull, indeed, rose supreme that day, for many of its gallant lads gave their all.'

Jack Harrison, a teacher and rugby player for Hull FC, was one such killed during the Oppy Wood battle. A German machine gun was playing havoc amongst the platoons. He ordered his men to shelter in a shell hole, courageously rushing the machine gun, singlehandedly. As he hurled his bomb at the German crew his men saw him fall face down, but he had stopped the machine gun, allowing them to advance. He was posthumously awarded the Victoria Cross for his bravery and sacrifice, his wife Lillian receiving it for him in 1918 from King George V.

So many men lost their lives in this battle that for years afterwards Oppy villagers would not enter the wood, believing it to be haunted.

Shelia Burr's granddad, John Busby (born in 1889), and his brother, Walter Busby, both signed up to fight in the first wave of recruitment in September 1914, when the call for Pals battalions was given. They were two of a family of thirteen children, but their mother died within two days of giving birth to John, so he and Walter were raised by their neighbour, Emily Bogg. John was born with a caul over his face which, for fishermen, was an amazingly lucky omen! He married Annie Elizabeth in 1907, aged just 18. John joined the 3rd Hull Pals Sports Battalion, becoming a lance corporal, and Walter joined the 11th Tradesmen's Battalion. Unfortunately both boys were killed in action. John was involved in the Battle of Arras a few months after he had been home to Hull on leave. He and his wife had three children by then and she was pregnant with a fourth. As he kissed them goodbye he had tears in his eyes, as if knowing he would never see them again. There seemed to be a common sixth sense about whether one would come through the war or not and John must have believed his time was up. He never met his fourth child, whom Annie named Walter Arras, in memory. John died on the first day of the battle for Oppy Wood in May 1917, having been previously wounded in the Somme but not badly enough for a discharge. Annie had also tried to get him home at one point with a telegram informing him of his daughter's pneumonia, but compassionate leave was denied. Annie, heartbroken at his death, put a mention of him in the *Hull Daily Mail* roll-of-honour column every year until the day she died.

The Oppy Wood battle raged for a further fifty-five days and it was during the assault on 28 June that Walter Busby was killed.

The premonition of death or survival definitely seemed a common one. Gerald Dennis talked of a great friend of his, John Barker, who suspected his time was up:

John and Annie Busby on their wedding day in 1907. (Courtesy of Shelia Burr)

He had had the most vivid presentiment ... he was going to be killed in the next stunt ... 'I want you to take charge of these three green envelopes and post them for me when you come out of the action.' To this I replied that there was more chance of my being killed ... he was adamant and handed to me the three letters: one was addressed to his parents, one to his girlfriend and the third to the Vicar. I failed to cheer him up and I could not get him to change his mind, yet he was not miserable or even scared. John Barker's premonition came true and he was shot dead in the next push, even though he had been in reserve and should not have been in the battle. Incredible and tragic that it had happened as he had dreamt.[50]

Walter Busby, wife Louie and family. (Courtesy of Shelia Burr)

In an opposite example early on in the war, in 1916, Cecil Slack, a former Reckitt's employee, wrote to his sweetheart, Dora, 'There is always a feeling that one may die at any minute; it's not exactly fear, but just a very strong feeling of "not wanting to". Somehow I think I am to come through the war. I have always thought so.'[51] He was right.

The 1st Hull Heavy Battery Royal Garrison Artillery was posted to fight German East Africa, now Tanzania. The Germans were posing a real threat to the British Colony and troops were needed to push them back. Their experiences there should not be forgotten, as the conditions, aside from the fighting, were treacherous. Malaria, black-water fever and typhoid claimed many victims and there were other enemies, such as the jigger flea, ticks, rhinoceroses, crocodiles and tigers. The army did not conscript men as they were unable to implement normal leave but, ironically, unaware of the dangers, many men volunteered for East Africa. Rupert Drake[52] gives a detailed insight into the conditions the men faced during their time there, with diary extracts concerning tarantulas and snakes in their tents, severe rains, giraffes who became entangled in their telegraph wires and the very real problem of dysentery. By November 1917 they had finally cleared the area of German forces, but of the original 274 ranks who had gone out just 61 returned, only to be posted to France in July 1918.

George Saul was one such Hull man who served in the German East African Campaign. His son remembered him coming home once with a piece of 9in-long ivory and ostrich feathers: 'I remember him laying down in front of the fire shivering yet covered with blankets … my mother … told me he had malaria fever.'[53]

The East Yorkshire Regiment arrived at Salonika in 1915, engaging the Bulgarian forces in battle. At the beginning of 1918 the Allied troops there were preparing for a major offensive intending to end the war in the Balkans, but the British did not play a major part until the September. This is one theatre of the First World War that many people do not know existed and countless lives were lost in the battles fought here.

Mrs Constance Collins's father, George Hemsworth, was a signaller in the West Yorkshire Regiment. He was one of three brothers to serve in the war. Walter Hemsworth joined the 2nd Battalion of the East Yorkshire Regiment aged just 17 and was killed only three months before the end of the war, in August 1918. Mrs Collins showed me an article reporting his death:

George Hemsworth, signaller with the West Yorkshire Regiment. (Courtesy of Mrs Constance Collins)

News has been received that Private W. Hemsworth, East Yorks, was killed in action ... while serving at Salonika. The deceased soldier was the son of Mr and Mrs G. Hemsworth, of 98 Somerset-street, Hull, and prior to the war he worked on the office staff of the National Radiator Company. He was only 19, and enlisted at the age of 17. His two brothers are serving with the Minesweepers. In his memory his parents placed the following in the paper; In loving memory of our dear son, Pte Walter Hemsworth, killed in action at Salonika ... He sleeps with England's heroes, in the watchful care of God.

The East Yorkshire Regiment war diary from this period states that on the 25th at 0030:

Party of Enemy 10 to 15 strong approached the Advance Post on HILL 380. Enemy were fired on and bombs were thrown at them by our men. Our Adv. Post withdrew down the C T to SPI for a distance of about 40 yds and took shelter in a shell hole and opened fire on the enemy. Enemy threw one grenade and withdrew. Grenade fell in the shell hole occupied by Adv. Post killing 2 and wounding 2 O.R. Advance Post was re-occupied and patrol sent out.

The dead man's penny Private Walter Hemsworth's family was sent after his death. (Courtesy of Mrs Constance Collins)

This was in all probability the account of Walter's death.

Gallipoli, the Dardanelles, was another theatre of war in which the East Yorkshires suffered heavy losses. As in East Africa, the soldiers had to face unusual threats aside from the enemy, flies and dysentery being prevalent, the 'Turkey Trot' weakening the men and making conditions harder still. It is estimated that the British Army lost more than 29,000 men during the Gallipoli campaign, the Turkish Army more than 60,000 and still the peninsula was not conquered, the campaign finally being abandoned.

One soldier explained in *The Snapper* what a terrible time the East Yorks had been having in the Dardanelles:

We started from Witley 980 strong, all ranks. Now (September 1915) we have 362, so that we have lost over 600 … in about seven weeks, and mostly in about five days of fighting. I, frankly, do not expect to survive another show like that. I should not be at all surprised if we were shoved up again, as there are no fresh troops here. But keep cheerful, and try and get people at home to realise what this means – the bravery of an aching heart. And the more people realise the terrible waste of life and limb … the sooner will they clamour for the means to finish off this and all wars.[54]

Private Arthur Austin Lamb, 1st 4th East Yorkshire Regiment. (Courtesy of Pat Bratton)

The 1st 4th East Yorkshire Regiment saw their fair share of bloodshed at Ypres and many met their end through the treacherous use of gas. The diary of Captain B.M.R. Sharp described the events at the Battle of St Julien: 'the men never faltered but went on and on – a splendid sight – they did magnificently, hungry and tired and weary tho' they were.' These Territorials certainly upheld the proud tradition of the regiment in this, their first battle.

Pat Bratton's uncle, Arthur Austin Lamb, signed up in Beverley to the 1st 4th East Yorkshire Regiment in April 1914, aged just 16. They trained in the Londesborough Barracks in Hull and were part of York and Durham Brigade, Northumbrian Division. Arthur had been in training at Deganwy army camp when war broke out and his regiment was brought back to Hull on 4 August. The war diary from this time shows hasty medical inspections were carried out the next day and then defensive entrenchment along the East Coast was commenced. On 13 August, when the call was given for volunteers to serve abroad, 75 per cent volunteered. They received their first inoculation on 30 September, the second on 8 October. By April 1915 the battalion had been ordered to France, arriving late the night of the 17th.

Pat has a letter written to Arthur from his mother, dated 21 April 1915:

> My Dear Son, I have just received your postcard and see you have arrived safely at your destination … Auntie Madge … would have liked very much to see you before you went but she is hoping like me, that we may have you safely home again in the near future. Don't forget your prayers Dear, no need to tell you to do your duty. I know you will do your very best for King and Country … Now Dear don't be too reckless and daring. I know just how impulsive you are. God Bless you my Boy and grant a speedy victory over our enemies and that you may all come safely through this terrible time … Fondest love and hopes for your speedy return from your loving Mother.

Tragically this letter was returned home unread as Arthur was already dead. The young lad had died on the first day of fighting for his regiment, at the Battle of St Julien, on 24 April, a mere seven days after arriving in France. The battalion war diary at this time recorded that four days after the unit had arrived in France, the enemy attacked at Ypres and the battalion was 'rushed to the horror of gas warfare. On their first day in action – the first time they had even seen a battlefield – the Battalion lost its Commanding Officer, Second-in-Command and 95 men.' Arthur was reported as 'missing in action' and his heartbroken mother would check the ships of soldiers coming home every time. Pat told me that Arthur's sister, Dolly, contracted a fatal case of meningitis and on her deathbed she apparently said 'I'm coming, Arthur' and then their mother knew he was dead. She checked the ships no more.

On 1 July 1916 the Battle of the Somme began. In the first hour 564 of the 750 Grimsby Chums who went over the top were killed or wounded. By the end of the day only a hundred or so remained.

A Young Man He Was

A young man he was and in his Prime
When he answered to the Call
And went to join up with his Pals
At the City Hall

A young man, yet old enough
To sire a breed of three
And soon another on the way
That he would never see

Off to France to beat the Hun!
See the World! Have some fun
Home for Christmas – might as well
And what a tale we'll have to tell
our Grandchildren in years to come

His brother went along with him
To keep the Pals' end up
There'd never been such merriment
Since Rovers won the Cup

Young men both – to see the World
They saw the Somme.
And when all that was done
They saw the fields of Arras' plain
They were no longer young

That bright May dawn,
the Line advanced
Walk, my lads – don't run
Behind the Creeping Barrage
That would wipe out every gun.

How far he got, we'll never know
With the Company of Pals
For by next day the brothers lay
Somewhere in No-Man's-Land
Men dying, calling,
crying for their Mothers
As their blood ran in the Earth
No use for you to cry, my Lad
Yours died to give you Birth
A rare birth yours, Dear Grandfather
A magic caul upon your face
Your Mother wept to see
A truly lucky Omen,
in a Town that went to sea

John Busby's family, including baby Walter,
1917. (Courtesy of Shelia Burr)

Our Grandma bore her grief, her pain
With dignity and Grace
Her son, she named him Walter Arras
But never saw the place.

We made the journey for her
And in her name we stood
In the place that had been
No-Man's-Land
Affront of Oppy Wood

Known unto God his only stone
For he was never found
Perhaps he still lies buried

Beneath that worthless ground
Perhaps one day they'll find him
It happens now and then
And he'll have a Soldier's burial
And be Known unto Men
But you'll have to hurry up Young Man
If this you mean to do
For there's not many of us now
Who will remember you.

He was not old our Grandfather
As Grandfathers are old
It was not Age that withered him
As his memory grows cold

(For John and Walter Busby of the Hull Pals, killed in action,
May 1917 at Oppy Wood. Poem written by Sheila Burr, 2007)

In a speech made by Field Marshal Sir John French in May 1915, he strongly commended the East Yorkshire Regiment for their heroic work during the Second Battle of Ypres, 'which will rank among the most desperate and hardest fights of the war … the Germans tried by every means in their power to get possession of that unfortunate town … that mean and dastardly practice hitherto unheard of in civilised warfare, namely the use of asphyxiating gases.'

Private Francis Dukes wrote to his mother and the letter was published in *The Snapper* in August 1915:

> I was gassed twice … it made my eyes bad and I felt very sick … the gas, when you first smell it, is like the perfume of some flowers, and you are rather tempted to take more than is good for you, as it tastes rather sweet at first. It is like mustard flowers, mixed with some others.[55]

At the door of each billet a soldier was stationed every night to warn the others of gas attacks. He was to strike a hanging shell case with his bayonet if he saw it coming, but, as one soldier commented, 'how do I recognise whether it is gas or just smoke?'[56]

Margaret Hardcastle's great-uncles wrote about some of their experiences of gas:

> 09/09/1916, from Will
> We came down from the line yesterday for a few days rest … had a pretty rough time up this time. Had my first experience of gas: Rotten Stuff – had to wear our smoke helmets for a long spell. Don't want anymore of it!

> 17/10/1917, from Harold Ward, 17, no. 2 Gen.
> milit: Hosp, Old [Oak?] Park, Canterbury. Dear old sports, No doubt you will have heard I am back in dear old Blighty once more. I got a dose of old Fritz's gas on the 2nd & had to go into hospital on the 9th after sticking it out for a week. Its damn queer stuff & you can't detect it unless you hear the shells coming ever as they only go off with a little pop & the gas does not affect you until some

time after. I lost my voice & very nearly went blind & had a rotten cough & pains in the chest & was in a rum state when I became a stretcher case. Things are all right here & am glad to say am very much better, my eyes are still a little misty & I have to keep stopping writing & my voice is of the husky order but the pains have nearly disappeared & my cough is getting 'apologetic' so I have good reason to be thankful I am in my present billet, which is distinctly of the variety known as O.K. I can imagine you saying 'well, he always was one of the gassy sort' but don't you believe it, no more gas for me if I can help it. Hope you are all in the pink & H.M. 'Babs' still going strong. Has Willy – I. Am been home on leave yet? No more just now. Yours gassily Moses. Xxxxxxxxxxx

Private Laurence Sawyer. (Courtesy of Mrs Carr)

The small box respirators were first issued in 1916 and many were made in Hull's Reckitt & Sons' factory.

Mrs Carr's grandparents had three sons, John William, Sidney Mawson and Laurence Sawyer. Laurence, or Lock as he was known, was Mrs Carr's father. He served as a private in the King's Liverpool Regiment and John, nick-named Jack, was an acting bombardier in C Battalion, 317th Brigade, Royal Field Artillery, 63rd RN Division. Jack would have trained at Wenlock Barracks, Anlaby Road, joining up in August 1914. He died in the Third Battle of Ypres in October 1917. He was awarded the Territorial Force War Medal, the third rarest medal to be given in the war and his name is on the Passchendaele memo-rial list. His brothers both survived the war, Laurence having sustained an injury at one point, but being sent back when

John William Sawyer. The Imperial Service Badge shows that he volunteered to fight overseas. (Courtesy of Mrs Carr)

he was better. He went on to run his own fruit and vegetable shop after the war.

Jack Oughtred gave a snippet of what the Battle of Passchendaele was like:

09/10/1917 My Darling, I fear that it is a long time since I last wrote to you – nearly a week – but I have been over the top as O.C. and not without some success. It was quite the hottest stunt that I have ever been in on the whole ... the shelling was simply hellish ... we gained all objectives and took heaps of prisoners. The Battalion won great fame for itself by the way it carried on. Some of the sights I have seen there I'll never forget. We were 48 hours without any food or water and had to collect it off the dead – my lips are still cracked and broken with the lack of it.[57]

Dave Carrick's great-uncle, Arthur Carrick, was a private in the East Yorkshire Regiment. Born in 1890, he was in his late twenties in the First World War. Dave remembers visiting his uncle when he was a child and used to love listening to his stories, while sitting by the coal fire. Dave said his uncle would become very emotional, often welling-up, when telling his tales from the front. He saw, as all did, many of his friends die and lived through some awful conditions. He talked about the cruel trench conditions, how bitterly cold it was in winter and how some of the men would urinate in their clothes, as much as a way to keep warm as anything else. He was wounded by shrapnel on his back and used to show Dave the scar. Arthur was involved in the Battle of Passchendaele, which, as a child, Dave thought sounded very romantic, and he remembers his uncle talking about the terrible gas attacks and how it made them extremely sick. Arthur was captured by the Germans and taken as a POW, growing vegetables in a prison camp until the end of the war. When the

Arthur Carrick.
(Courtesy of
Dave Carrick)

Armistice was declared, apparently the German guards threw down their rifles and walked away and all the prisoners downed their gardening tools and walked in the opposite direction, home. Arthur went on to live a long and happy life, dying, aged 91, within hours of his wife's passing.

Alan Duckles' father, Amos, referred to as an errand boy on the 1911 census, age 15, joined the Territorial Army around 1913. His father was a boiler maker, his brother being his apprentice, his sister a general servant, and his other sister an umbrella maker. Born in December 1895, Amos was 18 when war was declared. He joined the 1st 4th East Yorkshire Regiment, then transferred to the Army Cyclist Corps at some point in 1915 and went abroad to fight, later moving to the Devonshire Regiment. Amos's mother was a very house-proud lady and Alan remembered the story that, when Amos was home on leave, she would make him get

So many Hull Pals were lost in the ferocious battles during the war that soldiers were replaced by men of other regiments. By 1918 the Hull Pals casualties were so high that the 12th and 13th battalions were disbanded and the remaining men used to strengthen the 10th and 11th battalions.

91

changed in the shed right at the end of the garden as he was so filthy from the trenches! Amos survived the war, suffering a wound to his ankle which was not bad enough to return him to the ever-sought-after 'Blighty' and he continued to the end. He married Elma Key, whose brother, Edward, was also fighting in the war, with the Northumberland Fusiliers. Unhappily Edward was not so fortunate as Amos and was killed during the second week of April 1918. When the family were sent the dead man's penny remembrance, they also received a letter with some details of how he died:

> Our reports show that … 5 Northumberland Fusiliers were engaged in the fighting South of Ypres … where the Germans made their second great attack of that spring … One man in the Battalion says: 'We were near the River Lys in front of Merville, on April 10 when the Germans broke through. We had to get out of the trench and run for it … That evening we took up a position further back, and several of us were lying together behind a hedge, when a shell came over and all but myself were killed.'

Amos Duckles, on the gun, stationed at Deganwy training camp, sighting the gun on Cardigan Castle across the bay. (Courtesy of Alan Duckles)

George Bleasby's father, Thomas Lavender Bleasby, was a lance bombardier in the 1st Hull Heavy Battery Royal Artillery, in the 67th Divisional Ammunition Column. He joined up in October 1914 and was stationed abroad by 1916. He was a shoeing smith before the war and his talents were used for the first two years in the Hull Heavy Battery. He told George that he remembered the Prince of Wales visiting the trenches and offering all the lads a cigarette. He was wounded in Ypres, being sent home, never to return to the front. George showed me some X-ray pictures of his father's skull and leg, with pieces of shrapnel embedded in them. The damage to his leg plagued him all his life but he went on to run his own fruit and vegetable business, Bleasby's General Store, in Marmaduke Street. George's wife, Mary, had two uncles who fought in the war: Henry and George Leonard Bell. Both were privates – Henry's service number was 33064 and George's was 11429. Sadly both boys died in the war: George in April 1915 and Henry in March 1918. Their brother, Horace Albert Bell, Mary's father, was not well enough to fight in the war, but saved the letters he received from his brothers. George Bleasby showed me one written from Henry eight days before he died, just months away from Armistice Day:

Above left: *Private Amos Duckles, 1st 4th East Yorkshire Regiment. (Courtesy of Alan Duckles)*

Above right: *Edward Key, Northumberland Fusiliers. (Courtesy of Alan Duckles)*

 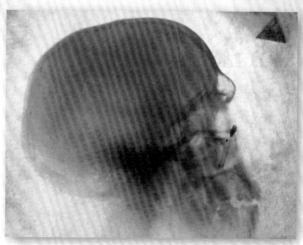

Above left: *Private George Leonard Bell. (Courtesy of George Bleasby)*

Above right: *Thomas Bleasby's shrapnel wounds, shown on an X-ray. (Courtesy of George Bleasby)*

Thomas Lavender Bleasby, 1st Hull Heavy Battery. (Courtesy of George Bleasby)

Wednesday March 20th 1918
Dear Mother and Father,

I expect you will be rather unsettled on account of not having heard from me for such a long time. Of course you know the reason, I have not been able to write. We have done a [the next bit had been scribbled out, probably due to censorship] and during that time we were unable to write. You cannot get letters censored, so I sent you several field cards, so you would not be so anxious. We are at [censored] reserve and I hope shortly we shall be out for a rest.

We had very decent weather whilst being in the line, although it was rather cold during the night. I had my first wash yesterday morning of several days, which I greatly appreciated.

There are a lot of Hull men in this batt. and I am among a very decent set of fellows. I was talking to a Hull man who had just returned from leave. He says you had unwelcome visitors a few days ago [reference to the Zepplin raid in Hull]. I am very sorry to hear this and trust you have recovered from the shock. I thought you had finished with this trouble. I guess Aunt Frances would be very much excited. When I hear from you I shall learn all the interesting news.

Well I hope you are all keeping well. Be of good cheer and don't worry should you not hear from me for a few days, don't get alarmed. You will know I am not in a position to write. I will not cause you unnecessary anxiety.

I am in the pink of condition (although I am fed up) and am sweating on an early peace. Roll on duration.

Don't get alarmed but keep on smiling, and pack all your troubles in your Old Kit Bag.

Remember me to all various friends.

Heaps of love
Your loving son Henry

Private Henry Bell.
(Courtesy of
George Bleasby)

Letters from home kept the boys at the front going but likewise letters home were a lifeline for loved ones who could but wait.

One lad writing to his father from France told him how, 'I was hit over the heart and my glass saved my life – my steel shaving mirror. Mary's photo. was shattered, and my cheque book. My Cardigan was torn, but my shirt and body were not touched. Anyhow, I got up and carried on until we were relieved.'[58]

What a letter to receive!

Lilian Rudd's husband's granddad, William, was a sergeant in the 7th Battalion of the East Yorkshire Regiment, aged 25 when war broke out, and William's father-in-law, John Hoggarth was in the same battalion with him, aged 41. Lilian has a letter sent from John to his wife, Mary Jane, dated 20 December 1917:

Dear Wife
Just a few lines to let you know me and Will is in the best of health, hoping to find you all at home the same.

I have just received the xmas cards and I think they are very nice. I have just showed Will them, we have just be having tea together. We are in no man's land but thank god we are all right. I am sorry I carn't [*sic*] even send a card in return but I might be able to send Jim a new year gift. We haven't had any pay for a month now, and if we had we could not spend it because we are miles away from any inhabitants. I don't know what sort of weather you are having at home, it is horrible out here, you would pity the poor boys if you seen them, if fact I am as bad myself, I carn't even get a fire going on a morning for the wind and snow and then I have to be careful the Germans don't see the smoke or else I would get shelled. He is not satisfied shelling, he comes round bomming (sic) us. I don't know how you feel at home when he comes Bomming. I know he puts the wind up us but I will tell you my old 2 of [illegible]. I will be glad when it is all over but I still keep as happy as a young 2 year old yet and I am the oldest man in the Batt, the boys say I am made of stone and I believe I am well [illegible] I thank you Kate and Jonny very much for the cards. Well I will say good night and God bless you all. So no more at present, from your loving husband.

Sergeant William Rudd, 7th Battalion, East Yorkshire Regiment. (Courtesy of Lilian Rudd)

The end of the letter is very touching, he signs his name and writes *WISHING*, all in tiny kisses, then 'you all a Merry Xmas and a Happy New Year Good night and God bless you all'. Tragically just one month later John passed away. He died of pneumonia in France, hardly a surprise considering the conditions he mentions in his letter. His son-in-law William helped to bury him and one can barely imagine how he must have felt. William survived the war. He was awarded the Military Medal in September 1917 and commended for action:

> During a raid upon the enemy trenches north of Rouen in the [illegible] July 28/29, this NCO took command of the half company attacking the 2nd objective north of the railway cutting after his officer was killed and led them forward with great determination and courage. He took the trenches, killed the enemy and withdrew according to programme. This party brought back 6 prisoners and he displayed great courage and initiative throughout. This NCO has been on active service with this Batt for two years.

The men and boys from Hull certainly did our city proud, with their bravery and sacrifices. The conditions they had to live through are such as no one should ever have to endure, but the thought of home and Hull was never far from their minds:

> We were all a bit sentimental and when someone said that from Cassel Hill top the white cliffs of Dover could be seen on any bright day, quite a number of us strolled the five miles there to see if it were true. We never did see … our own country … but it was pleasant to think that Blighty was not so far off.[59]

As Harold Tesseyman put it in a letter home in 1917: 'Well, old sports, no more this edition. Keep on keeping on & we'll have a beano some day. The last 10 years of the war will be the worst! Au revoir. Xxxxxxx for t' young 'un.'

5

Keep the Home Fires Burning

Whilst the boys at the front were risking their lives for King and Country, the people left at home in Hull were fighting their own war, with food shortages, rationing, Zeppelin bombings, constant news of the death of loved ones and many disruptions to their lives.

The first Zeppelin raid on Hull struck just before midnight on 6 June 1915.[60] Kapitänleutnant Mathy, the commander of Zeppelin L9, was apparently attempting to reach London but by the time he reached the English coast the winds were against him

Zeppelin damage to Edwin Davis', viewed from the roof of Holy Trinity church. (Courtesy of Hull Museums)

Zeppelin damage, Market Place, Hull, June 1915. (Courtesy of Hull Museums)

and he could not reach his target. Instead he followed the railway lines to Hull and launched a twenty-minute attack, the first two clusters falling over densely packed working-class housing areas, then more in the Old Town and Drypool, resulting in twenty-four deaths and many others being injured.[61]

Edwin Davis' drapery store was set on fire and Holy Trinity church suffered some damage, as well as many houses, a school and a furniture warehouse.

Steven Suddaby[62] quotes Marion Large who remembered the first Zeppelin raid on Hull, even though she was a small girl then:

> I remember being carried down the stairs by my father … the devastating crunch of bombs falling, the shaking of the house and the clatter of glass as our back windows cracked and fell are unforgettable … it was long before we dared go back to bed … our little world was shattered and for me, childhood was over.

The HMS *Adventure*, a navy ship in repair in Earle's Shipyard, had been the only defensive response the city gave. Although not the first raid on an English town, this was the worst attack in terms of material damage and casualties. The authorities were unprepared and manpower was scarce due to the number who had enlisted, but both the police force and fire brigade were called out to help.

The shock of a German attack on home soil brought forward the reality of war in ways that even the mass exodus of young men could not. To know that loved ones were not safe in their own beds gave more impetus for men to join up and fight the 'dirty Hun'.

The outrage and anger felt caused rioting in the city in the early hours and many German shops were targeted. The Corporation later received notice that eighteen separate attacks had been made prior to 5 a.m., German shops and houses having windows and doors smashed and possessions looted. One of the most serious incidents happened outside a butcher's shop in New Cleveland Street. It is estimated that a crowd 700 strong gathered outside, overwhelming the police and soldiers called to the scene, demolishing the shop-front and carrying off most of the belongings.[63]

Zeppelin damage to housing in Waller Street, June 1915. (Courtesy of Hull Museums)

Prior to this, feelings towards the Germans were sour, especially after 16 December 1914, which witnessed a terrible tragedy when Scarborough, Whitby and Hartlepool were bombarded by shells fired from a German fleet, killing 137. Next the infamous sinking of the British ocean liner RMS *Lusitania*, on 7 May 1915, caused further uproar amongst the civilians of Britain. Of the 1,959 people on board, 1,198 died, 885 of whom were never recovered.

The reaction to these events was reflected in an article from the *Eastern Morning News* on 10 May: 'The time has come when we must treat all Germans as our deadly foes. Too long we have been parleying with the enemy within the gate. We must begin our warfare at home … We must look upon the Germans as people not to be trusted.'

Even the sermons preached at certain churches around Hull encouraged retribution for such 'animalistic' acts, especially after the arrival of forty *Lusitania* survivors on 12 May.

Although viewed as a great tragedy, political advantage was drawn from the *Lusitania* incident in the shape of propaganda. British posters appeared to encourage enlistment, such as the picture of a mother and baby sinking beneath the waves, the word ENLIST standing alone at the bottom. Another encouraged people to 'Take Up the Sword of Justice', with a picture of the listing *Lusitania* in the background. To propel the public passion further, a rumour was spread that German schoolchildren were given a day off school to celebrate the sinking of the *Lusitania* and the German propaganda Goetz medal, depicting the sinking, was used in England as proof that the attack was premeditated, as the date stated 5 May.

With Hull being such an important port, it attracted many immigrants and by the 1890s Germans had formed the largest immigrant group in the city. There was a German Working Men's Club, German churches and even a German political club: Club Freiheit. Following the aforementioned atrocities, hatred against anyone with a link to Germany or with a German-sounding name began. Johan Herman Ellermann, who moved to Hull around 1850, and Georg Friedrich Hohenrein, who opened a butcher's shop in Hull in 1850, both married English girls but became two examples of naturalised Germans who were victimised.

Lusitania *propaganda medal and box. (Courtesy of Hull Museums)*

As an important port Hull was a Zeppelin target in the war.

On 6 June 1915: 24 killed.
On 5/6 March 1916: 9 killed.
On 9 August 1916: 10 killed.
On 25 September 1917: 3 killed.
On 12 March 1918: 1 killed.

By the end of the war over 1,500 British citizens had been killed in air raids.

Many German families adopted English surnames in an attempt to avoid attention, Max Schultz's taking his wife's maiden name, Hilton, with the Hohenreins becoming Ross.

Alderman Henry Feldman, a member of the Hull Corporation Finance Committee, was criticised for advocating free school meals for children whose fathers had been recruited. His German-sounding name made people suspicious that it was a German plot to undermine the city's finances.[64]

Voices of Hull[65] includes another example of a Hull family who had a clock in the kitchen with a German eagle on the top and when the father was wounded in the fighting, the mother yanked the eagle off and threw it in the fire, such was her resentment of the Germans!

German houses and shops were stoned and raided, with hostile, intimidating crowds sometimes several hundred-strong gathering outside these premises. Threats were called, especially from women whose husbands or sons had been killed in the war, but, unlike other cities in the country, no injuries were sustained.

D.G. Woodhouse[66] believes that the impact of the war was harder on the fishing community of Hessle Road than other districts in Hull and that drinking increased in this area, adding to the problem. Some 300 trawlers and their crews had been requisitioned and the steady loss of ships and crews was devastating.

The rioting had a substantial impact on the Hull German community and many of the businesses closed for the duration of the war. Hohenrein and Son was one such business, which declared temporary closure in November 1915 'in consequence of the erroneous opinion of many of the public that we are Germans or Naturalised English'. The family, naturally, felt disappointed and upset that they were being subjected to – as they saw it – unfair treatment by the people of Hull, and stated 'it is a distressing decision to come to after sixty-odd years of unbroken trade'. They even went so far as to offer £500 to any local charity if anyone could prove that they were not English.

After the first Zeppelin attack a gun was mounted on the roof of Rose, Down's and Thompsons for added defence in addition to air-raid buzzers and blackout rules. This included the top parts of the street lamps being painted Oxford blue, the lower areas Cambridge blue – the effect being that little light was reflected upwards – as well as windows on trams having paint and curtains, with two blue lamps to light inside. When the buzzers were sounded all light had to be extinguished, including the striking of matches in the street, with heavy fines being imposed for any who breached regulations. Of course, with these night visitors, the ever popular and brightly lit Hull Fair week had to be discontinued for the first time in its history. Hull became known as 'the darkest city in the Kingdom'.[67]

Rumours abounded as to what could attract the Zeppelins, with ideas that the ticking of clocks or even whispers could be heard from these cigar-shaped monsters in the sky.

The second raid, this time meant for Hull, was the next March and became known as 'The Snowy Night Raid'. The blackouts were no use this night, as a layer of snow highlighted the city. In addition to other damage, the glass roof of Paragon Station was destroyed and many families fled towards the countryside to escape. Seventeen people died, with many more injured.

Three incendiary bombs dropped from a Zeppelin in Woodmansey parish, March 1916. (Courtesy of Hull Museums)

105

Mrs Hall recalled a man passing by her house, asking for a glass of water. As he entered the house 'what a shock we got – he was saying "Goodnight" to his sweetheart when the bomb fell, killing the girl in his arms; he was covered in her blood'.[68]

As the Zeppelin passed down the river she was fired on by the *Killingholme*, but to no effect, and although eyewitness reports say the Londesborough Barracks searchlight had caught the Zeppelin in its beam there had been no response from the installed gun on Rose, Down's and Thompsons. Frustration and anger led to more disturbances, including the stoning of a Royal Flying Corps vehicle in Hull and the mobbing of a flying officer in Beverley.

Citizens were further outraged to eventually discover the gun mounted on the roof of Rose, Down's and Thompsons was a wooden one, erected as a deterrent and morale booster, as there were insufficient funds to set up a real one. Gunners had been ordered to appear to be on duty from 8 p.m. until 5 a.m. and they made a show of cleaning the weapon, fooling both Germans and Hull folk alike. Sir Alfred Gelder, the MP for North Lincolnshire, apparently became so incensed at the authorities for attempting to trick the public with this dummy gun that he raised the matter in the House of Commons. More rioting and lobbying ensued and so four real anti-aircraft guns were mounted around the city, along with searchlights.

The next attempted raid in April was unsuccessful due to the defences, which were highly praised in the *Hull Daily Mail*:

> During the most intense period of air raids in Hull, from May 1915 to November 1916, there were forty nights when the buzzers sounded – that averages out at one every other week. Such fear would have taken its toll on many lives and businesses.

'The engagement was a magnificent spectacle. The population kept cool, and watched the firing with confidence. In one part of the town every shot from our guns was greeted with a murmur of applause ... the monster turns tail.'[69]

The city was not so lucky in August, however, when a further nine were killed and twenty injured in another attack, the Zeppelin staying out of range of the guns. This was not the last raid on the city, but many others were deterred by the new defences.

Mr Reed recalled hearing bombs falling on the allotments near his house:

The allotments were at the end of a small street called
Whitworth street, and every house in the street had its
doors and windows blown in … the following morning,
I went and looked at the crater the bomb had made, and it
was about 6 meters deep and 10 meters long.[70]

People were not really sure how best to avoid the threat of the
Zeppelins. At first such tactics as hiding under the kitchen table
or in an airing cupboard were employed, then people started to
gather in open areas such as West or Pickering Park or nearby
fields. 'One night when the buzzers blew, we were all in the house.
My father made us all go out into the street and lie in the middle
of the road on our stomachs.'[71] With the first few attacks people
would congregate in the streets when the alarm sounded, to see
what was happening and eventually the raids became quite a
social occasion. Crowds could be seen making their way to open
areas, laden with bank books, snacks and blankets. The Hull
Corporation allowed schoolchildren the next day off to catch up
on sleep if the 'release siren' was blown after 10 p.m., which many
saw as an exciting bonus.

*Zeppelin bomb
dropped in Hull in
1917. (Courtesy of
Hull Museums)*

T.B. Heald recollected the air raid of 5 March:

> I remember seeing outlined against the starry sky the
> dark cigar-shaped outline making for the coast. In the
> morning damage and death. After this when raids came
> people went to the country/open air spaces, thought
> this was the best chance for safety. People could be
> seen trekking along the main routes out of Hull, family
> by family – mothers pushed perambulators containing
> babies and precious belongings, fathers, if not fighting,
> carried toddlers in blankets or looked after the older
> kids – a sad sight indeed.[72]

Zeppelin damage,
Collier Street,
March 1916.
(Courtesy of
Hull Museums)

The warning buzzers were given nicknames as the people became
more used to hearing them. One situated at Blundells Spence was
called 'Lizzie', another was 'Clara Butt', after a deep-voiced singer
of the time, another 'Mournful Mary'.

The special constable force was a great asset to the city during the raids, patrolling the streets and assisting people where necessary, enforcing blackouts and DORA regulations, fighting fires and generally engendering calm. They were also responsible for checking all vehicles entering and leaving the city, as well as escorting aliens in the city's ports, on Dock Guard patrol. They were men generally too old for military service or those not eligible for enlistment. Hull claimed the proud distinction of raising a force of over 3,000 unpaid special constables.

The local authorities also did their bit to help the townspeople, lobbying the government for funds for air-raid insurance, helping those made homeless find new places to live, employing tramway men to pick up women and children for free when the 'All Clear' buzzer sounded and the Lord Mayor personally paid for the funerals of some of the victims of the raids.

Harold Wright was 15 during this time and remembered the panic that the Zeppelins brought with them:

> … but perhaps my most vivid recollection of the affair as a whole is the incident on the night after the raid. It had created a great deal of anger and tension and on the Monday evening in Cleveland Street the police were out to control the crowds. Then an old lady wearing an apron was allowed through, she walked calmly along the street. Nobody was taking any notice of her. Then suddenly she pulled a flat-iron from under her apron and flung it through the window of a German pork butcher's shop. Immediately this set the crowd alight. They broke through, knocking the police aside, and all made for the shop. People were running down side streets carrying meat.[73]

The deaths of the British men on the E13 submarine in August 1915 added to the general anti-German feeling in the country and especially in Hull where the victims were brought ashore and the city became the scene of one of the largest and most moving funeral processions of the war.

Brass buzzer used at Blundell and Spence as an air-raid warning. (Courtesy of Hull Museums)

Zeppelin damage, Queen Street, Hull. (Courtesy of Hull Museums)

The anti-German riots eventually died down, but people were still very suspicious of any German-sounding residents, believing them to be spies, signalling the Zeppelins, especially as they were not bombed themselves. Of course, the German citizens thought of themselves as English and were deeply upset by the reaction of the town's people. D.G. Woodhouse gives the example of Lawrie Kohler who attempted to sign up to join the navy:

A Girls Working Party was set up by Reckitt's employees who produced 3,772 sandbags, 1,240 socks, 370 scarves, 200 shirts, 87 belts, 424 mittens, 138 cuffs or gloves and 59 helmets. The sum of £709 was given for parcels and cigarettes and £176 for the Prisoners of War Fund from Reckitt's workers.

The P.O. looked at me in horror. 'Are you a Jerry?' he asked. 'No!' said I. 'I was born here in Hull, but my father was a German.' 'Well,' said he, 'we don't want no Jerries in the British Navy.' I am sorry to say that I immediately burst into tears … the injustice of the world about me … I wanted to give my life to the Nation. The Nation did not want it.[74]

The last Zeppelin raid on Hull occurred on 12 March 1918.

The adversity of the war often brought out the best in people, as they banded together to help one another. One lady remembered an incendiary bomb setting their coalhouse on fire and 'people – strangers – started coming into the house and taking furniture out and putting wet sheets up at the walls to stop the fire spreading.'[75]

A number of the large businesses in Hull also did their bit, providing warm, 'safe' shelter to the families of their employees, within their buildings, during air raids. Thomas Ferens opened up his stables as a refuge. Even the Boy Scouts had their role, passing messages in raids and acting as stretcher-bearers.

Home air defence was a major concern for the government at the outbreak of war and they increased the number of military aerodromes. As a result, 179 acres of Beverley Westwood were requisitioned in the East Riding in 1915, the aerodrome buildings being located just to the west of today's racecourse buildings.

A ground force was also necessary and East Yorkshire was the only county in Britain to provide as many as five specialist units of a volunteer force, the Horse Transport being the only one of its type in Britain. This unofficial home defence force, many of whom were men too old to enlist, originated in rifle clubs. As War Office backing was not forthcoming, donations were given from the East Riding County Council and Hull Corporation, to arm the corps with rifles and a uniform. By July 1916 they were officially recognised as the East Yorkshire Volunteer Force. In the event of an invasion their job was to guard strategic points, including coastal areas, and delay enemy advance.

Another significant group to arise were the Wagoners' Special Reserve, formed by Sir Mark Sykes of Sledmere, and included some of the first men to go abroad driving the horse-drawn wagons with supplies of food, fodder and ammunition for the front line. They were farmers of the Wolds, specially selected for their driving abilities, and became part of the Army Service Corps.

Soldiers on leave arrived in a country very different from the one they had left. Gerald Dennis commented on some of the changes:

I could not help noticing that there were trials and difficulties at home. The so-called white bread was poorer than the Army ration bread. Coupons were required for meat of all kinds and for sugar. Housewives queued up for this, that and the other. My coupons were added to the others of the household and the tin of bully that I had brought with me was welcomed.[76]

Home leave was often a haphazard affair. Some soldiers got none for two years, then would have two in six months, but whenever it was, it was undoubtedly a particular highlight. David Bilton quotes one soldier describing home leave:

Came the happy day when I found myself in possession of all the necessary papers, leave pass, 'clean' certificate, on my way across country to … a train which carried me … to England … to be in an English train was wonderful and still more so to be in London … but most wonderful of all was my arrival in Hull and re-union with my family and young lady.[77]

However, many stories of home leave are tinged with sadness that the people at home could not comprehend or imagine what life was truly like at the front.

When Corky came home on leave in August 1917 his sisters asked how things had been:

… straightaway I could tell that I was going to meet the same old problem of them not understanding what it was really like. I, like others, found out that you could only talk of the war with those who really experienced it. So what you did was drop in to 'stock phrases' such as, 'oh it's all right, a bit hot sometimes, but not all the time'. You said this when really you wanted to tell whoever you were talking to of how really awful it was to see young men dying or blown to bits, or of your own terrors and fears. But whenever you did talk this way to whom so ever you did, they seemed to lose interest and become a bit uneasy as if they were talking to a mad person, who might suddenly become hysterical.

When he finally turned in he 'was uncomfortable in the bed and inexplicably I found myself wishing that I was back in France with the lads.'[78]

Corky mentioned later that after talking to other Tommies back in France his experience of home leave was a common one.

Gerald Dennis described when he came home on leave, arriving into Paragon Station:

… at the barrier were scores of people – fathers, mothers, lovers and even children awaiting loved ones … A grand welcome home, and hundreds of questions about the front to which I gave evasive answers as I had no wish to pile on a description of the horrors of war. We talked for hours. At long and happy last they retired and I went to the bathroom. No standing up under a shower of warm water for a few minutes followed by a cold douche this time, no race against time, but just reclining at ease. Months had passed since the last visit to an Army shower … and then into a soft feather bed with clean sheets as a covering, warm all over with no need to put my legs into the arms of my cardigan in order to get extra warmth. Yet I was restless and tossed and turned over and over again. I had heard men say that when on leave they had to get out of their beds and sleep on the floor, and now I could understand this.

Of course I ran into old friends. They were all well-meaning when they came up, hands outstretched, and asked: 'How long are you here for?' or, more usually, 'When do you go back?', 'Have you killed any Germans?' or 'What's it like out there?' We weren't in the same world. I suppose that whatever answers we gave to the more serious questions were not believed, how could these people grasp the horrors?

THE WOODEN GUN THAT SAVED HULL

'Hull Famous! A lurid Zeppelin account. Wooden Gun Humour.' This article appeared in the *Hull Daily Mail* on 13 March 1919, documenting the view of Hull presented to the people of Chicago:

Hull has been famous in many ways all through its history, and now the Great War is causing fresh honours of notoriety to be thrust upon us ! The American Press is devoting itself to details of the struggle gleaned in European centres, and Hull, of course, is receiving its share of attention. The following despatch by Mr Edward Price Bell in the *Chicago Daily News* ... will be read with interest not unmixed with amusement in the city. It is headed:- GREAT WOODEN GUN ON ROOF SCARED OFF HUNS AND SAVED BRITISH TOWN. Hull, England, January 20th – This is the story of the wooden gun that saved Hull and the shipping of England. The ancient mariners along the quays of Hull chuckle when they relate it. Month by month the story grows. When the last soldier is demobbed the story will have become one of the legends of the war. And when you ask a native of Hull to tell you something about the Zeppelin raids that terrorised the city for three years he will omit many details – the details of the women and children and old men who died of terror in the streets, of the scores who were blown to atoms while in their beds, of the thousands fleeing in the dead of night through the streets into the marshes and the fields. He will omit these things and with a smile tell you that the British Government played a great joke on the people of Hull by placing a wooden gun on top of a building and making believe it would fight off the Zeppelins.

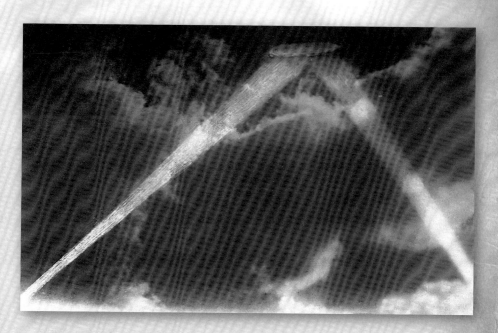

Zeppelin caught in searchlights. (Courtesy of Hull Museums)

He also made mention of how important the munitions workers back home were, as the lives of the boys at the front depended on having shells. They were outraged when they heard about strikes for more money '… we felt we ought to let them know that we could not strike, not even for more shells, let alone more money. Needless to say, we were all disgusted with them. They did not have to worry daily about their lives.'[79]

With so much propaganda and pressure, both nationally and locally, to join in the war effort, those who spoke out against it were a resounding minority. Each town had its own share, as did Hull, but their voices were lost beneath the rush for enlistment:

> Although patriotic feeling has been roused to concert pitch, I venture, as one voice speaking in the wilderness, to claim that Britain has made a mistake in not remaining neutral. Britain's attitude should be strict neutrality, and to use her power to influence the other European countries to cease hostilities … and to urge them to settle all differences … by a conference of representatives of the various countries concerned. Then indeed Britain would be truly great.
>
> Will you kindly allow a space to protest against the war. Why are so many people dumb on the question of peace? Do we not all want happiness? But the road taken by this Government leads to unhappiness, misery and starvation to the majority of our people.[80]

Conscientious objectors had differing reasons for not wanting to fight in the war. Many held religious convictions that forbid them to take another's life, for some it was political and, for a small minority, it was just an excuse[81]:

> Quakers and the Military Machine. The Society of Friends … appreciates the attempt of the Government to meet the case of conscientious objector in the Compulsory Service Bill. We must, nevertheless, make clear the fact that … a large number of conscientious

objectors are not prepared to accept compulsory service, whether combatant or otherwise, under the military authorities. To attempt to compel persons holding these views to accept service required by the military authorities for the successful prosecution of the war would, in our opinion, be a violation of freedom of conscience. Objection ... based on the belief that human life is sacred ... nor can the objector assist in any way the conduct of war by such an alternative service as mine-sweeping, because in that way he is aiding the military machine whose function involves the destruction of life.[82]

With compulsory recruitment looming, pacifists campaigned for a 'conscience clause' in the 1916 Conscription Act for the right to claim exemption from military service. Over 16,000 men made that claim but had to attend a tribunal assessing the sincerity of their claim. With bias and patriotism a dominating factor, more than 6,312 conscientious objectors were arrested.

Whatever their reasons, conscientious objectors were generally viewed as cowards and non-patriots. For some, like Frederick Sherwood, who was an International Bible student from Hull, it was acceptable to contribute to 'work of national importance', such as building airfields, making munitions or being stretcher-bearers. For others even this participation in the war effort insulted their morals and refusal led to harsh treatment and alienation. Reg Jolliffe, an insurance clerk and Congregationalist, refused any such participation and spent over two years in Hull Prison.

The *Hull Daily Mail* reported in 1916 that the Port of Hull Labour Committee was coming up against objections to conscientious objectors working at the docks: 'Considerable friction has been caused among the trade unionists on the docks owing to the introduction of men holding tribunal exemption certificates – i.e. conscientious objectors.'[83] The paper reported that there were protests against the issue of such certificates and appeals to the Committee to revise such cases. In the case mentioned here, the 'man in question was going to take up agricultural work' but it was stated that it was difficult for conscientious objectors to find work.

The same paper told of a man who had appealed at a tribunal that he was a conscientious objector but that the appeal was dismissed and he was given 'time': 'He was taken to a camp and was stripped naked. A rope was tied round his waist, and he was dragged and frog-marched round the camp; he was then "ducked" in a dirty pond eight times, and at the ninth time he gave in.'[84]

It was stated that there were some men who were not really conscientious objectors, they just objected to military training, but that was still no justification for inhumane treatment and those with real objections had a right to their consciences, without being subjected to 'such diabolical wickedness'.

Another report noted that Sir James Reckitt had asked the Lord Mayor to look into the matter of alleged serious ill-treatment of a number of soldiers who:

> ... had conscientious objections to military service. Sir James, who is a Quaker, referred to members of his own family who had grievously suffered by reason of their religious objections to military service. So far back as 110 years ago, he said, an uncle of his had served sentence of imprisonment in Lincoln Gaol for his convictions, and even in those far-off semi-barbarous days one term of imprisonment was deemed sufficient to expiate the charge. He regretted to learn that to-day the conscientious objector was being subjected to repeated terms of imprisonment for the same offence.[85]

Not all the news was doom and gloom. The *Hull Times* reported the joyous occasion of a:

> ... second visit to the Port of Hull ... within three years ... by Their Majesties King George V and Queen Mary. Medals and other honors were distributed to 173 officers, non-commissioned officers, and men. His Majesty was evidently impressed by the record with which the sons of Hull and district have made glorious our page in the war.[86]

The royal visit was accompanied by thousands of spectators and large displays of floral bunting and the king spent valuable time with the injured soldiers in the VAD hospital.

6

COMING HOME

When I come home, and leave behind
Dark things I would not call to mind,
I'll taste good ale and home-made bread,
And see white sheets and pillows spread.
And there is one who'll softly creep
To kiss me ere I fall asleep,
And tuck me 'neath the counterpane,
I shall be a boy again –
When I come home!

(Poem by Hull man Leslie Coulson,
who died of wounds, 8 October 1916.[87])

In a special edition of the *Hull Daily Mail*, published at 11 a.m. on
11 November 1918, it was proclaimed to be:

A SUPREME MOMENT It is officially announced that
the armistice with Germany was signed this morning.
The bloodshed is over. The strife is done. It is a moment
which fills the heart with unutterable emotion, but the
profoundest tendency among many of us will be to
thank God for it upon our knees. Our first thoughts, after
that, will go out to our sons, husbands, and brothers on
the sea, and in the field. We may be sure that their joy
is inexpressible. They have conquered! They have won

the war! Britain has laid down over a million precious lives, but they have not died in vain. May the noble spirits and souls of the righteous gaze upon our flags of rejoicing – may it be sober and seemly everywhere – and of victory today. It is finished! The 'Great War' is over … the supreme task is achieved, and we are fighting an embattled people no longer.

The war, which was supposed to be all over by Christmas, had finally ended. Celebration and rejoicing was seen throughout the whole country and as T.B. Heald remembered, Hull city centre was in uproar while crowds surged around the statue in Queen Victoria Square, singing and dancing.[88]

Mrs Latham recalled the huge parties that were thrown in Hull after the war:

> … with tables all down the street and decorations. I used to have a photograph where I had one of my brother's uniforms on – all the young lasses got dressed up in uniform. We had all the windows and the doors decorated, and the particular terrace where I lived was nearly filled with relations and there was a great big blank wall. My eldest brother chalked and painted on it the King and the Queen and Union Jacks. It lasted ever such a long time.[89]

Elsie Swift also remembered the street parties in Hull. She was 12 then, living in Bean Street, and recalled the flags and bunting. 'Her grandmother sat in a wicker chair: spread out before her on a table was a table-cloth she had made which featured the flags of all the allies.'[90]

For the people of Hull the Armistice meant a getting back to normal life, a return of some of their brave sons, brothers and husbands, but for the men themselves, it took a while for the reality to sink in.

When news of the Armistice reached the Hull battalions many sources say it was met with a surprising lack of enthusiasm,

Hull street party celebrating the end of the war. (Courtesy of Hull Museums)

the men merely turning over in bed for more sleep. There had been so much speculation over the duration of the war, so many rumours amidst the censoring that the soldiers were not sure what they could believe. They were too exhausted and disillusioned to show much response, at first, not to mention the fact that the war life was all they now knew. As Gerald Dennis put it:

> The news was too good to be true. I failed to grasp the significance of it and for a time could not adjust myself to it – I felt numbed. There didn't seem to be an appropriate way of celebrating; there was a little hand-shaking, but no shouting or cheering. It was left to those well away from the fighting parts ... to go wild with joy.[91]

Jack Oughtred relayed the news to his sweetheart on the 9th:

> We are all very excited at the news – the prospect of the armistice. It does look hopeful, dear, don't you think so? Anyway, we shall know by 11 am Monday. Just fancy, Peace. I'm trying not to build too much on this Peace idea because if it didn't come off it would be such a blow.[92]

Then on the 10th:

> I feel very bucked today with the good news. The Kaiser abdicated and the Crown Prince renounced his claim to the throne. We are all wondering if the Armistice will come off tomorrow.

Finally, the 11th:

> Well, dearest, isn't the news simply great? I couldn't sleep last night wondering if we should get the armistice. About 12 Midnight I heard cheering in the streets but we didn't get it through officially until about 9 am this morning. You ought to have heard the cheers. I never saw such excitement. Honestly, darling, I can hardly realise that to all intents and purposes the WAR is OVER. It's too much to grasp all at once. I can imagine what excitement there must be in England tonight. It must be tremendous. We are very quiet here, but very happy.

On the 12th the *Hull Daily Mail* expressed what the folk at home were feeling: 'The whole country gave vent to its pent-up feeling yesterday when the news of the signing of the armistice by Germany was received … [a] note of reverent thankfulness mingled extensively with the more light-hearted expressions of joy. It was a day of national goodwill.' It also reported Hull's rejoicings on the 11th:

> Since 9 o'clock groups of people assembled in Whitefriargate, anticipating the arrival of the anxiously awaited news … It was with especial gratification that the public heard the pealing of church bells which have been for so long silent. At 3 o'clock the City Square and its approaches were crowded with throngs of excited young people mainly. Crackers were let off in the streets, and horses and vehicles were decked with flags and streamers … Whitefriargate, too, was thronged with light-hearted crowds … The familiar sounds of buzzers

Hull street party, 1918. (Courtesy of Hull Museums)

were heard, now, however, not as dark warnings, but as heralds of joy.

Things were quieter at the front:

> There seems to have been great excitement in Hull about the Armistice – far more than out here. We had no cele-brations of any kind. The men just mentioned it casually in their letters too … on the morning of the 11th we were on the move. You could hear the guns pounding away as hard as they could until 10.59 – when they suddenly stopped. It was very weird – many of the men thought that we were pulling their legs.[93]

The declaration of the end of the war was very much a bitter sweet occasion. So many had lost their lives or their loved ones. Society had been shaken to its core. Killing, the ultimate taboo, had become the norm out at the front, how could these men suddenly return to civilian life or cope with normality after living for so long under such terrible conditions? The war changed everyone and everything.

Pat Bratton, whose uncle Arthur Austin Lamb had been killed in his very first battle, aged just 17, recalled her grandmother telling her of when Arthur's friend, Harry Hutchinson, visited her after the war was over. He told her how 'they had to fill us full of whiskey to go over the top' and how the men all 'cried like babies for our mothers'.

The terror, the horror, how could the people at home understand it? The war may have been over, but for thousands it never left them. Shell shock, a condition not even properly recognised, afflicted many of the soldiers, following them home after the war, but who today could be surprised, knowing what they went through.

Corky gave such a description of one man the RAMC rescued:

One of the 'nervously exhausted' patients had a very bad night last week. He had a nightmare that was so severe in its effects that I thought he might go mad and harm himself. Whatever, it was proof that he wasn't 'swinging the lead'. He has got into this state before and has had to be restrained. Although he disturbs the rest of the ward, they are not critical or scornful. They sympathise with his condition and tell of how he was buried in mud for days under constant bombardment. When he was pulled out he was in a terrible state, unable to speak, trembling from head to foot and having completely lost control of himself.[94]

Jack Oughtred experienced a similar thing with a fellow officer in January 1916:

Three nights ago one of them [he only had two officers left with him at this point] went off his head for about ¾ of an hour. We all tried to calm him and at last succeeded. An 8in shell burst 15 yards from him during the day and I suppose gave him rather a shock.

In another instance Jack and his men were hard at work digging at night when:

A man with me ... lost his nerve when they started shelling us a bit on the way up. We had hardly started out before he was shaking like a leaf and after a 100 yds or so he fell down and grovelled at the bottom of the trench.

I of course sent him back with another man to look after him. Not his fault really I suppose, but a thing like that takes away the spirit of the men very quickly and also has a little effect on yourself.

Again in April:

I unfastened the coat of one of the wounded. He said he was dying but I told him not to be such a damned fool. Almost before I got his coat undone he gave a sigh and his head went back. His wound was in his leg. He must have died through shock I imagine. Two men also were struck deaf and dumb. Another lost control of himself and climbed over the parados and hared off across country. He was killed up at the support line. One of my men when he saw the wounded and dead lying as they were all over the place ran down the communication trench and has not been seen since.[95]

Corky recalled a horrific incident that stayed with him. He was with a large troop of soldiers during a short night march towards Cambrai when all of a sudden they were attacked from planes above dropping bombs on them:

I watched in horror as men were blown high in the air or bombs blew men in all directions on the ground. It seemed that the awfulness of it would never end … then there was an awful silence. Then the cries, screams, groans and shouts of the wounded filled the air. Pulling ourselves together, out of the shock that the terrible events had put us into, we went amongst the jumble of broken, shattered and disinte-grated bodies and slipped and slid on blood that was flowing on the road as if a short shower had washed it. By the time ten minutes were up we counted seventy six casualties, out of a hundred, most of them fatal. Those few men who were not

> Hull was known as 'the door-step to Blighty' for the 80,000 British prisoners of war who travelled through our port on their way home.

hurt were shocked into immobility and some became hysterical. ... For days and days afterwards I could not close my eyes to sleep without the terrifying business rolling round my head like a cinematograph.[96]

Mrs Allen from Grimsby remembered that her father had been gassed during the war, as well as being wounded in the hand:

He went back to Marshall's but he could only do a brush job because of his crippled hand. There were six of us children then and we saw some of the terrible effects besides his physical wound. He used to have dreadful nightmares. He would wake up screaming ... he was always fighting. Anything that moved, curtains, anything, he'd be getting up to fight. We had no Armistice celebrations inside or outside the house.[97]

Unfortunately this reaction was not uncommon. Barnes mentions two Hull Pals whom he interviewed describing their difficulty at readjusting when they returned home. They were 'nervy and unsettled' and Weasenham and Pearson spoke with bitterness of Lloyd George's "land fit for heroes" and found only unemployment as they returned to a world greatly changed from the one they knew.'[98]

Before they even got home the soldiers at the front had to undergo the painfully slow process of being demobbed, which included travel details for home and sourcing work for them once they were back in Britain. Many of them had a long wait to get back to the families and home they so eagerly sought.

The Battle of Estaires took 120 Hull Pals' lives. The Battle of Oppy Wood took 209 men from our battalions, topped only by the Battle of the Ancre, which in total claimed 263, 140 of whom died in one day, on 13 November.

Margaret Hardcastle's great-uncle William Tesseyman expressed the views of the waiting men in a letter home in January 1919: 'It doesn't appear as though I shall get away now for some time as the demob scheme seems to be pretty well in a muddle! I expected to get away last Sunday – so I shan't worry about it, for I shall get away before very long.'

He still had not moved a month later: 'I didn't intend writing any more letters for I thought I should have been home by now. I really think I shall be coming in a few days time, almost for certain. Too excited to write so excuse me. Your loving brother Will.' His demob papers show he still had to wait another month before coming home.

Oughtred described the wait, saying how education classes had been set up:

> They are trying to form classes here to instruct all ranks in their former civilian occupations. Rather a big job to tackle. I've had to send a return in about everybody – what they were before the war and so on. All the officers here have to fill in a form saying what job they intend taking up on being demobilised. That has rather 'stumped' me. One Battalion in this Brigade has already sent some 100 of its men – miners – home.[99]

Many of the men who left work to fight at the front were promised their jobs would be left open for them when they returned. Alan Duckles' father, Amos, was given this opportunity, as Alan showed me in a letter from his father to his mother in January 1919:

> My Dear Elma, Well love I have fairly good news for you. I have received a letter from my old boss at Sandersons saying he is willing to give me my old job back again. So I have given it in to my Battalion orderly room and I do not think it will be long before I am on my way to Blighty for good.

However, many trades and industries struggled to recover after the war, thus adding to the mass unemployment of so many men returning at once. The land fit for heroes was not quite as expected.

The soldiers were not sure what to expect when they returned, as Jack Oughtred illustrated:

THE HORRORS OF WAR

It seems a wonder, after the horrors and constant fear the troops had to endure on a daily basis, that there were not more men who deserted, although, of course, if they were caught, the it would mean certain death. There is only one recorded case of such a desertion from the Hull Pals; Private Charles McColl from the Tradesman Battalion. Lieutenant Slack was responsible for putting together a firing party, after McColl had twice run away and was then tried and sentenced. Sergeant Len Cavinder was in charge and of the ten chosen for the execution, five had blanks in their rifles, in an attempt to give the men some peace of mind about having to execute one of their own, one who was said to be clearly unfit for military duty. B.S. Barnes gives a moving account in *This Righteous War* (pp146–51), showing how such forced actions terribly upset the men and the outrage that soldiers felt about the whole business. McColl was clearly suffering from some sort of shell shock, and they were loath to act against him, but in the First World War such conditions were barely understood nor even recognised. 'Everybody who took part in it was affected. It was a terrible thing to usher a man into eternity whether it was law or not. No it was a sorry affair all together … that was the worst thing that happened to me personally.'

10th Service Battalion training at Wenlock Barracks in 1914. Relaxed, eager and excited, no one imagined the horrors to come. (Courtesy of Hull Museums)

I've ceased worrying as to what I'm going to do when I come home for good. Things have altered so. There must be a lot of good jobs about, and after all these years of fighting out here I feel that I have a right to one. There are many people in England who I think don't realise how the war has changed the men out here. The men for instance feel that they've risked their lives out here for years – and now that the Hun is beaten and the war over they expect some return from the country – and, dearest, they are right to expect it.

Whether they could handle 'normal' jobs again was another matter, even Jack stated he did not want his old job back. 'I see that immediately demobilisation starts one may apply for leave providing that you have a job to go back to … no more Bank for me. I'm not stopping in the army either.'[100]

B.S. Barnes gives an example of one Hull man, Walter Edward Smith, who did return to his job at Reckitt's in 1919, but 'found the life too claustrophobic after the army'.[101]

The employment situation was indeed dire, and affected women too. They had discovered a new independence during the war and were pushed out of jobs so that the returning soldiers could find employment. Even many of their previous jobs, such as laundering, were given to disabled ex-servicemen. Life after the triumph of the long-awaited peace was hard for everyone.

In Hull, from an estimated 70,000, 7,000 men and women had died in the war and 14,000 were disabled. A War Trust was set up to aid those whose lives had been irrevocably affected and by 1927 1,040 people had received £74,000 between them.

As the war progressed it became ever clearer that many of those men fortunate enough to return home alive would be disabled to some degree and jobs for all ex-servicemen would be scarce. The government developed a scheme of providing smallholdings for such men, one of which was situated at the Crown Colony at Patrington, Sunk Island.

The authorities also set up the City of Hull Great War Civic Trust to aid disabled ex-servicemen and the dependents of those who had been killed. This charity lasted for sixty-five years.

Ship believed to be carrying British POWs home. (Courtesy of Hull Museums)

There were also plans for a Victory Hall in Hull and many companies who had sent the majority of their workforce out to fight gave returning soldiers financial help. Reckitt's was one such firm, distributing £8,000 amongst their employees who had served in the war.

St Dunstan's worked to aid Hull's blinded soldiers and sailors returning, 'to train these men to earn a living by the development of other faculties, to maintain their self-respect'[102] and Welton Hall became an important convalescent home.

There was also a Kitchener's Memorial Fund established to help disabled officers and men of the army and navy, and the Hull Trust Fund provided houses, farms and jobs for those who needed help.

When finally the men did start to return home, as well as being very instrumental in helping its returning citizens, Hull was the gateway for thousands of others, travelling through our port en route:

Homecoming Prisoners. Over 17,000 Have Passed Through Hull. Today was one of the busiest in dealing with returning British prisoners at Hull. Seven trains were arranged to dispatch the men to Ripon and the officers to Scarborough, from whence they will be sent to their homes. The greatest enthusiasm prevailed. Men, overcome with emotion, exclaiming fervently, where they stepped ashore, such remarks as 'Four years this is what I have been waiting for' … 'One foot in Blighty.'[103]

Homecoming scenes were always joyous and emotional for everyone. Even the king sent blessings to Hull men, as this surviving letter shows:

Memorial to Jack Harrison, Hull KC stadium. (© Susanna O'Neill)

Private Vivian Tidy, who served with the 4th Battalion, East Yorkshire Regiment, had been taken as a prisoner at some point during the war and his family recently revealed a hand-written note he was sent from King George V shortly after the Armistice. 'The Queen joins me in welcoming you on your release from the miseries and hardships, which you have endured with so much patience and courage. We are thankful that … back in the old country you will be able once more to enjoy the happiness of a home and to see good days among those who anxiously looked for your return.'[104]

Our own newspaper, the Hull Daily Mail, ran numerous narrations on the welcome and celebrations for returning soldiers:

Home From Battlefield Hull Welcomes Its Warriors Cheering Crowds Line The Route. The haunting strains of the band playing 'Home Sweet Home' fell pleasantly upon the

Street Party, Hull, 1918. (Courtesy of Hull Museums)

ears of the Hull men of the 92nd Brigade as they marched with martial gait through Hull on Monday. They were returning at last to good old Hull … By 10 o'clock crowds began to assemble along the line of the route, and an hour later there were thousands … on the wall of the Guildhall … were the words, 'Well done, Hull.' … The Lord Mayor addressed them; 'Men, you have fought a fight; you have gained a victory; you have won a peace. I may sum up all I wished to say in two words, Thank you. I give you a very hearty welcome from the citizens of Hull.'[105]

From June 1919 when more troops arrived:

The 1st East Yorks. was welcomed back to the depot at Beverley this afternoon with great rejoicings. An official welcome was also extended by Lord Nunburnholme … and other prominent townsmen. Beverley was, of course, gay with flags and bunting, and the townsfolk were most enthusiastic in their welcome. The band of the Vol. Batt. East Yorks. arrived from Hull and joined in the musical honours accorded in the march to the Guildhall at Beverley, where Alderman Wray … gave a reception. Afterwards there came the triumphant march to the Barracks … where a real homecoming had been prepared.[106]

Still the celebrations rang out late July:

Hull on Saturday observed, happily, with dignity and fitting decorum, and with the rest of Britain, the day appointed for the celebration of peace and the victory of our Forces … the ringing of merry peals on the bells at Holy Trinity … the city was gay with flags … with fireworks, bonfires, children in fancy costumes, and music … and a memorable military and naval procession.[107]

Emma Keeitch remembered the Armistice festivities:

We borrowed forms from the school and had them all down the middle of the road and hundreds of kiddies were seated there, all dressed up. The committee had got a nine-gallon barrel of beer in our room for the men. We had decorated the doorway with electric lights from the Christmas tree and we took the piano into the street and we kept the party going all night and all next morning. It was smashing, and smaller parties continued for a while as different ones got home. Mind you, they talked about coming back to a country fit for heroes and there was no work and there was no money and there was no help. Things were very, very bad.[108]

Some 346 executions of 'deserters' occurred during the war. Many of these men suffered severe shell shock but were tried and sentenced by courts of junior officers, their cases seldom being accurately presented. The British Army believed a system of control governed by fear was essential for proper discipline to be maintained.

One of the most tragic occurrences at the end of the war was that of the influenza epidemic, which stole more lives than the war itself. As Corky stated in June 1918:

We are busily occupied with an outbreak of influenza. It takes all the heroism and glory out of war (if there is any in it in the first place) being ill or even dying from a disease like influenza. We have so many patients it looks as if what was an outbreak of one or two cases is now an epidemic … The virulence of the influenza strain that infected us struck down an Army more effectively than bomb or bullet.[109]

Jack Oughtred also commented on it that same month: 'I heard from Mearns yesterday, and he says that 20 Officers of the 4th and 500 men are down with this "flu".'[110]

The *Hull Daily Mail* related a sad and not uncommon story from July 1919: 'A Tragic Home-Coming. Arriving at Grimsby, after a nine months' voyage, James Rivers, a sailor, learned for the first time that his wife and four young children, to whom he had written regularly, had all died during the influenza epidemic nine months ago.'

Along with the tragedies there were many joyous and happy reunions, many stories to be told and honours to be received. Margaret Hardcastle's great-uncle, William Tesseyman, was one of the Hull men who was awarded the Distinguished Conduct Medal, 'after helping to bring in the wounded under exceptionally heavy shell fire.'[111] His cousin, Cecil, also received the same and brother Harold received the Military Medal for 'conspicuous

Tesseyman family business premises, Land of Green Ginger. (Courtesy of Margaret Hardcastle)

Eton Street shrine, still visible today. (© Susanna O'Neill)

gallantry at great personal risk and devotion to duty'. All three cousins, Cecil, George and Walter, plus the brothers William and Harold, served in the conflict. When he returned, William took over his father's leather business, in the Land of Green Ginger, one of the oldest trades in Hull, set up by his grandfather in 1817. Others found what work they could.

Corky got home in mid-February 1919. As the train 'finally made a long flat curve along the River Humber to Hull' the soldiers in his carriage all wondered what was in store for them next:

> They would be back in their old jobs 'or know the reason why'. They would settle down with the 'girl they had left behind'. I kept my counsel. I thought only that I had come through it when many of my mates had not. I wasn't the man I had been when I went in.[112]

It would take a long time for some of the men to settle back into a home routine, others never could. However, the bonds forged between the men who had served together were never forgotten, many making the regular effort to meet up, year after year.

Peter Chapman talked of those of the Grimsby Chums who made it home:

> ... back in the community to which they belonged, their past, with all its horrors, had welded them into a league of private remembrance, the bond of experience beyond sharing with those who knew nothing of the trenches of the Western Front. Old soldiers – and in the main the Chums were still all in their twenties – are reluctant to break such strongly forged links. Thus they determined never to allow the future to dissolve the past and, on November 22nd met for dinner ... Old comrades ... united by ties beyond the comprehension of other men. They were to do so each year for as long as they were able.[113]

The war to end all wars was over, it is such a great pity that peace did not endure.

Postscript

Legacy

It is hard to see the purpose of war, but if during this period of trial we are drawn closer to our fellow-men and learn to sympathise in others' sorrows; if we are taught the value of self-sacrifice and gain fortitude; above all, if we stop to think whether our fair name as a righteous nation is justified and resolve, each of us, by clean and upright living, to answer in the affirmative and to have the God of righteousness on our side; then this dreadful war will have some compensations.

(Reckitt's Magazine, September 1914[114])

The war claimed 16.5 million lives, it lasted 1,566 days, with 21.2 million wounded. More than 65 million men from thirty countries fought, not to mention the civilians involved and the casualties sustained. Over the four years 750,000 telegrams were sent out to notify families that their relative was dead, as Britain lost over 900,000 military personnel. Another 2 million Britons were wounded. More than 192,000 wives had lost their husbands, 400,000 children had lost their fathers and half a million children had lost at least one sibling.

It is estimated that over 70,000 people from Hull served in the forces in the First World War. The Hull Pals lost 2,000 men and over 7,000 local men and women were killed, with 14,000 wounded or disabled. On average Hull

Less than forty Hull Pals were court-martialled for desertion between 1914 and 1918, an amazing figure, given the terrifying and tragic conditions the men lived with, in those four years.

received fifteen casualties every day of the war, nearly 70 per cent aged under 30, including 1,500 serving teenagers. Some 14,661 merchant sailors died during the war and nearly 1,200 of them were from Hull.

At least ten streets in Hull lost more than fifty men.

Once the initial celebrations and euphoria of the Armistice were over, life had to carry on. The losses felt by families and communities were deepened by the poverty, lack of employment, food shortages and political unrest in the country. In many ways Britain was in a poor state, an anticlimax for returning heroes and drudgery for the rest. However, the war had also produced many military advances and was responsible for many other developments, such as surgeons' techniques to treat burns and

'Fallen' – An art installation by Martin Waters, November 2013, of 12,000 poppies, to remember the fallen. Displayed in Holy Trinity church. (© Susanna O'Neill)

The Dansom Lane Roll of Honour, with thanks to Reckitt Benckiser for allowing me to take the photograph. (© Susanna O'Neill)

other disfigurements, hospital equipment, mobile telephones and, of course, it widened the horizons for women. Society had become more democratic, with previously under-represented groups, such as women and the working classes, becoming better organised and more powerful than before the war.

Street Shrine, Bellamy Street, Hull, 1919. (Courtesy of Hull Museums)

Perhaps it was not for nothing that the men lost their lives.

Street shrines and rolls of honour had become common-place within communities during the war. For example, the Walker Street Shrine alone featured over 300 names, but only a handful of these shrines now remain. At one time they were religiously kept with vibrant flowers, but it became difficult to keep them up to date, as the death toll was so high.

Many factories and businesses created rolls of honour for their fallen employees, but as generations moved on those great sacrifices were pushed into memory. The Reckitt's factory built a garden of remembrance at the end of the war, with a stone foun-tain featuring the figure of Sacrifice and it is wonderful to know that a ceremony is still held there every Remembrance Sunday.

The most lasting memorial in Hull is the Cenotaph in Paragon Square, which was unveiled in 1924 and has a moving ceremony on each Remembrance Sunday, to this day.

Reckitt and Coleman remembrance plaque, with thanks to Reckitt Benckiser for allowing me to take the photograph.
(© Susanna O'Neill)

For the centenary celebrations Hull's Paragon train station has been adorned with twenty memorial plaques to honour 2,000 men who departed the station between 1914 and 1918 and never returned. This, along with the annual Cenotaph ceremony, is a perpetual reminder of and tribute to those young men who went through so much.

One of the battles to claim the highest number of Hull men in one day was Oppy Wood. This attack is built into the history of Hull and a large stone monument was created in Oppy in 1927 to remember the brave men of Hull. When the war ended Hull donated money to the village to help rebuild it and the memorial is a reminder for both peoples. When unveiling the memorial, the Lord Mayor of Hull spoke these words:

> To the glory of God and in memory of all the men of Kingston upon Hull and local units who gave their lives in the Great War, and especially of those who were denied the honour of a known grave, I unveil this memorial in the name of the Father, and of the Son, and of the Holy Ghost.[115]

Hull Cenotaph. (Courtesy of Hull Museums)

Hull was the first Yorkshire city to commemorate its fallen sons with a memorial on French soil.

The first annual memorial service to be held at Holy Trinity church was given on the sixth anniversary of the brigade's attack on Oppy Wood, 3 May 1923.

The thousands upon thousands of crosses and graves scattered across old battlefield sites in France are thankfully kept beautifully by the War Commission, and have been visited by millions, some small comfort to those who lost loved ones. Many have inscriptions etched on to them from visiting relatives: 'Oh for the touch of a vanished hand, the sound of a voice that is still.'[116]

A pride for what these men sacrificed never faltered for that generation and duty was a strongly inbred obligation. Cecil Slack, and many of the men writing home, expressed this often. 'Remember this, my sweetheart, risks in plenty I have taken, but they have all been necessary to my duty, and because of you and my people at home I will be as careful as honour and duty permit.'[117]

One of the twenty memorial plaques in Paragon Station honouring the 2,000 men who departed the station in the war and never returned. (© Susanna O'Neill)

The Oppy Wood memorial. (Courtesy of Hull Museums)

It was due to this sense of duty and love for King and Country that many of the men volunteered in the first place, not because of some bloodthirsty lust for killing. Even amidst all the horrors and carnage of the front line, there was a respect and certain camaraderie between the British and German troops. Many of the men expressed anguish at having to kill these men, some mother's son, and much guilt existed long after the war. Hull man Albert Barker said it all: 'I didn't hate them, they were the same as us, we all did our duty.'[118]

British and German alike all suffered, all lost friends, all experienced the horror of killing another human being, with the threat of their own death perpetually hanging over their heads.

Barnes described how dreadful and demoralising the shelling bombardments were, especially when trapped in one position, not knowing if each passing second would be the last. It is little wonder the men who returned suffered with nightmares for the rest of their days:

ERECTED BY THE STAFF
IN GRATEFUL REMEMBRANCE OF
THEIR COLLEAGUES WHOSE LIVES
WERE LOST IN THE GREAT WAR
1914 - 1919

R.R. BARKER	E. YORKS	E. HILTON	E. YORKS
H. BARNBY	E. YORKS	S. HOWGILL	CITY LONDON
F.F. BARON	R.F.A.	C.E. JACKSON	R.G.A.
S.J. BEAN	R.N.	H. LOFTUS	E. YORKS
W. BOOTHBY	E. YORKS	S.T. MAYNARD	LONDON REGT
J. BROUGHALL	CITY LONDON	F.S. MONSEY	CITY LONDON
H. CARR	N.F.	A. OSBOURN	E. YORKS
A.W. CHARLES	R.G.A.	H.J. PAULSEN	E. YORKS
C.K. CLARK	LONDON REGT	W.H. POUCHER	R.N.
R.W. CLAYTON	LONDON REGT	T. PRICE	R.G.A.
J.J.O. CROWTHER	CITY LONDON	C. ROBSON	RIFLE BRIG.
F. DAVISON	E. YORKS	H. SELBY	E. YORKS
R.H. DAVISON	R.N.	H.W. SHANKS	M.G.C.
L. DONNELLY	E. YORKS	H.L. SHARP	W. YORKS
A.E. COODERHAM	R.F.A.	C.H. STANDLAND	R.N.
C. GOODILL	E. YORKS	W.E. SWIFT	E. YORKS
T. GRANT	R.N.	R.H. TASKER	E. YORKS
R.W. GRAY	R.G.A.	S.D. USHER	R.F.A.
T.H. GREEN	M.G.C.	H.H. WATSON	LONDON REGT
A.W. HARDING	R.E.	R.P. WHITAKER	R.G.A.
F. HARRISON	E. YORKS	A.E. WILES	R.E.
J.E. HASNIP	CITY LONDON	E.W. WOODS	E. YORKS
H. HEWITT	R.E.	C.W. WRAY	R.G.A.

UNVEILED BY THE
POSTMASTER OF HULL
MAY 1ST 1920.

LOCAL JOINT COMMITTEE
J. STEEKSMA,
SECRETARY.

The Hull Pals had gone abroad with visions of glory and brave deeds; these things were indeed achieved, but many paid the price by being blown to pieces, cruelly maimed or buried alive by high explosive. For these reasons all men feared artillery, and if they escaped injury the mental scars they received took many years to heal. Some never recovered from them.[119]

Barnes quotes from Private Graystone's diary, describing the scene after one battle in which the Hull Pals were involved in: 'This afternoon I saw the whole Battalion's dead. The bodies were laid out along the trench side just as they fell. I shall never forget the sight as long as I live. It was hard to look upon them, dear old pals.'[120]

Corky described the heartbreaking scene of the death of a close friend, Bert:

> I tried to find his wound, which he said was in his stomach. I struck a match to see but as soon as I did a machine gun from quite close opened up on us. I did have time, however, in the brief flare of the match to see a great hole under his arm. It was a cavity from his arm pit to his waist and it was wide and deep. I caught a glimpse through tattered uniform of splintered white rib bone, torn flesh, blood vessels and what must have been his lungs. I was horrified and all I could do was to try and plug it with the spare shell dressings I had in my pack. They just disappeared as bloody wads into his body.

Bert knew he was dying:

> 'Corky, me owd duck, write to me missus for me. When tha writes, tell me mam I allus loved 'er.' He began to shake from head to toe. Then he went rigid and, like a child, tried to lift his hands as if going into the arms of somebody. He cried out 'Oh Jesus Christ, Corky, this is it.' And then he died.[121]

Ronald Leighton, friend of Vera Brittain, wrote to her after his first five months in the trenches:

> Let him who thinks that War is a glorious, golden thing … let him look at a little pile of sodden grey rags that cover half a skull and a shin bone and what might have been its ribs, or at this skeleton lying on its side, resting half-crouching as it fell, supported on one arm, perfect but that it is headless, and with tattered clothing draped around it; and let him realise how grand and glorious a thing is it to have distilled all Youth and Joy and Life into a foetid heap of hideous putrescence.[122]

As Corky wrote:

> Death here, in this war, was not the rose-tinted 'going to sleep' of postcards and romantic books. This was a war of flying flesh, slashing metal and earth shattering bombs. What happens here doesn't have much to do with what they think at home. It is another world.[123]

Roll of Honour for Hull and Barnsley Railway. (Courtesy of Hull Museums)

The war was not a subject often talked about by returning soldiers and many women whose husbands and sons did return, did not like to hear talk of it. It was as if such a shocking and tragic event had so affected the psyche of a generation that they shut their minds off to it, or at least, as best they could. One of the only times that the men would talk of the horrors they had endured was during their reunions, which became a regular occurrence after the war. The bonds and camaraderie between the troops is one thing that could not die:

> I think that so little of the horrors and conditions of the Great War were known in the twenties because Tommies of the Front Line came home on leave and said nothing because they did not want to alarm their relatives. I am proud that I lived with … the finest men and boys I have ever known … in dugouts just below the barbed wire of No Man's Land and shared their danger.

> The end of the war did not and could not terminate the friendships that it had created, and few were the men others wished to forget.[124]

> I leave the battery for the dispersal centre at Cambrai. I felt more despondent at leaving the boys than I care to admit. We have gone through a lot together and quite a lot are still here who were in the battery when it was first formed.[125]

There is now no one left alive who survived and remembers first-hand this terrible war. Those men who fought could never forget, as Gerald Dennis admitted when interviewed in 1988. He said that even though he had trouble remembering events from the previous week, he could recall 'his war experience as though it were yesterday, though he would like to forget some things that happened so long in the past'.[126]

It is now our duty to these brave men to remember them and the sacrifices they made.

So much more could be said about the war, about the hardships these men faced, about their pride, honour and bravery, about the men and women of Hull who *did their bit* and of the sorrows and adversity they too faced. The terrible sea battles, such as Jutland, where many of our men lost their lives, need to be remembered; the minesweepers, the nurses, the long hard work and money donated for the war effort; the stories of the Hull German families, who were persecuted because of their family heritage. Hull man Max Schultz deserves a mention for the brave work he did, using his German influence and knowledge of the shipping industry to spy for our government, even though it cost him dearly in the end. 'I was a spy in Germany, and I am not only not ashamed of the fact, but am proud of the risks I ran in getting information which I may fairly claim has helped us win the war.'[127]

Roll of Honour, Wilson Line. (Courtesy of Hull Museums)

Hull man Sydney Carlin should also be remembered for his bravery and patriotism – even after losing his leg at the Battle of the Somme he insisted on serving his country, becoming an ace in the Royal Flying Corps until he was shot down and taken as a prisoner of war. This heroic man did it all again in the Second World War!

Unfortunately the boundaries of one book limit the extent to which facts and stories can be conveyed and so I urge all readers not to stop here, but to make use of the numerous other books dedicated to Hull's part in the Great War.

The First World War is a subject that has been extensively written about, each book concentrating on a different angle but all inevitably highlighting the great trauma and scar left on

The Hull city centre Cenotaph. (© Susanna O'Neill)

A display of poppies in Hull's Ferens Art Gallery on Remembrance Day 2014. (© Susanna O'Neill)

our world history. The books that have helped me compile this volume have been invaluable for personal insights and information, especially as our generation has no one left who was alive during those horrific years. I would thoroughly recommended anyone wishing to know more about the war to read these books and I thank the authors for their detailed research and efforts to preserve the memory of all who played a part in the war effort.

This book is written in memory of a generation who went through such hardships, grief, fear and uncertainty for our sakes. It is a legacy of the brave people of Hull and the Humber, a thank you and acknowledgement of their sacrifices and, along with all other such books written on the subject, an instrument to ensure that we do not forget.

Never would the thought have crossed the minds of all those teenage lads – so eager to sign up, with no conception of what lay ahead – that a century on their actions would still be making an impact on us. May it be that way always. Lest we forget.

ENDNOTES

1 Avery, Alan, *The Story of Hull*, p.48
2 *Hull Daily Mail*, 24/04/1917
3 Letter from Richard Wake, *Hull Daily Mail*, 07/08/1914
4 Bilton, David, *Hull Pals*, p.17
5 *Hull Daily Mail*, 08/08/1914
6 *The Snapper*, December 1915, p.240
7 Babington, Anthony, *For The Sake Of Example*, p.10
8 Poem signed T.I. from *The Snapper*, Nov 1915, p.230
9 Poem from Florence Howe, *Hull Daily Mail*, 02/11/1914
10 *Hull Daily Mail*, 07/08/1914
11 Sheppard, Thomas, *To Commemorate Peace after the Great War*, p.102
12 Sheppard, Thomas, *To Commemorate Peace after the Great War*, p.94
13 Quote taken from *North Eastern Railway Magazine*. Bilton, David, *Hull Pals*, p.21
14 Barnes, B.S., *This Righteous War*. p.28
15 *Hull Daily Mail*, 14/09/1914
16 Bilton, David, *Hull Pals*, p.20
17 October 1915, issue 10, p.202
18 Fairfax, Ronald, *Corky's War*, p.11
19 *Hull Daily Mail*, 05/08/1915
20 Dennis, Gerald, *A Kitchener Man's Bit*, p.3
21 *Hull Daily Mail*, 09/06/1916
22 Markham, John, *Keep the Home Fires Burning*, p.70
23 *Hull Daily Mail*, 28/04/1915
24 Markham, John, *Keep the Home Fires Burning*, p.91
25 The *Hull Times*, 07/04/1917
26 *The Snapper*, monthly journal of the EY Regiment, 1915, pp139–141
27 Sheppard, Thomas, *To Commemorate Peace after the Great War*, p.111
28 Markham, Alice, *Back of Beyond*, pp57–61

29 Barnes, B.S., *This Righteous War*, p.117
30 Markham, John, *Keep the Home Fires Burning*, p.92
31 Markham, John, *Keep the Home Fires Burning*, p.82
32 *Hull Daily Mail*, 24/03/1915
33 *Hull Daily Mail*, 02/02/1917
34 *Hull Daily Mail*, 09/06/1916
35 Markham, Alice, *Back of Beyond*, pp.57–59
36 Markham, John, *Keep the Home Fires Burning*, pp71–76
37 Wilkinson, Alan, *Destiny: War Letters of Captain Jack Oughtred M.C.*, p.13
38 Fairfax, Ronald, *Corky's War*, p.22
39 *Hull Daily Mail*, 29/05/1919
40 *The Snapper*, monthly journal of the EY Regiment, 1915, p.130
41 Wilkinson, Alan, *Destiny: War Letters of Captain Jack Oughtred M.C.* p.15. Letter dated 09/07/1915, before he was sent out
42 Barnes, B.S., *Known to the Night*, p.105. Corporal Nix account
43 Fairfax, Ronald, *Corky's War*, p.58
44 Barnes, B.S., *This Righteous War*, p.59
45 Barnes, B.S., *This Righteous War*, pp73–74
46 Fairfax, Ronald, *Corky's War*, pp59–90
47 Williams, Edward Stanley, *In the Pink*, p.17
48 Dennis, Gerald, *A Kitchener Man's Bit*, pp42–90
49 Barnes, B.S., *Known to the Night*, pp73–74
50 Dennis, Gerald, *A Kitchener Man's Bit*, p.92
51 Willatt, Dora, *Thank God I'm Not a Boy!* p.83
52 Drake, Rupert, *The Road to Lindi, Hull Boys in Africa*
53 Barnes, B.S., *Known to the Night*, p.90
54 *The Snapper*, p.184
55 *The Snapper*, pp112 and 151
56 Barnes, B.S., *This Righteous War*, p.53
57 Wilkinson, Alan, *Destiny: War Letters of Captain Jack Oughtred M.C.*, p.131
58 *The Snapper*, monthly journal of the EY Regiment, 1915, p.206
59 Dennis, Gerald, *A Kitchener Man's Bit*, p.141
60 Kimberley, Stephen, *Humberside in the First World War*, p.39
61 Hook, John, *This Dear Dear Land, The Zeppelin Raids on Hull and District*, p.10
62 Suddaby, Steven, *Buzzer Nights: Zeppelin Raids on Hull*, p.1
63 Woodhouse, D.G., *Anti-German Sentiment in Kingston Upon Hull*, p.49
64 Woodhouse, D.G., *Anti-German Sentiment in Kingston Upon Hull*, p.27
65 Wright, Trevelyan, *Voices of Hull*, p.118
66 Woodhouse, D.G., *Anti-German Sentiment in Kingston Upon Hull*, p.39
67 Markham, John, *Keep the Home Fires Burning*, p.13
68 Suddaby, Steven, *Buzzer Nights: Zeppelin Raids on Hull*, p.2
69 *Hull Daily Mail*, 06/04/1916
70 Suddaby, Steven, *Buzzer Nights: Zeppelin Raids on Hull*, p.7

71 Quote from Mrs McIntyre. Suddaby, Steven, *Buzzer Nights: Zeppelin Raids on Hull*, p.8

72 *Yorkshire Ridings Magazine*, p.18

73 *Decades Flashback*, issue 4, p.31

74 Woodhouse, D.G., *Anti-German Sentiment in Kingston Upon Hull*, p.83

75 Quote from Doris Gagen. Suddaby, Steven, *Buzzer Nights: Zeppelin Raids on Hull*, p.14

76 Dennis, Gerald, *A Kitchener Man's Bit*, p.187

77 Bilton, David, *The Trench. The Full Story of the 1st Hull Pals*, p.165

78 Fairfax, Ronald, *Corky's War*. p.146–47

79 Dennis, Gerald, *A Kitchener Man's Bit*, pp60, 186–87

80 *Hull Daily Mail*, 06/08/1914. Letter from M.J. Davis

81 *Hull Daily Mail*, 10/08/1914. Letter from H.E. Jenkins

82 *Hull Daily Mail*, 10/01/1916

83 *Hull Daily Mail*, 08/08/1916

84 *Hull Daily Mail*, 04/08/1917

85 *Hull Daily Mail*, 27/07/1917

86 The *Hull Times*, 23/06/1917

87 Barnes, B.S., *Known to the Night*, p.49

88 *Yorkshire Ridings Magazine*, September 1968, pp17–18

89 Markham, John, *Keep the Home Fires Burning*, p.63

90 Barnes, B.S., *This Righteous War*, p.128

91 Dennis, Gerald, *A Kitchener Man's Bit*, p.236

92 Wilkinson, Alan, *Destiny: War Letters of Captain Jack Oughtred M.C.*, p.228

93 Wilkinson, Alan, *Destiny: War Letters of Captain Jack Oughtred M.C.*, p.232. Letter dated 19/11/1918.

94 Fairfax, Ronald, *Corky's War*, p.76. Dairy entry dated 20/08/1916.

95 Wilkinson, Alan, *Destiny: War Letters of Captain Jack Oughtred M.C.* p.24/35/50

96 Fairfax, Ronald, *Corky's War*, pp234–35. Dairy entry dated 02/09/1918.

97 Markham, John, *Keep the Home Fires Burning*, p.63

98 Barnes, B.S., *This Righteous War*, p.157

99 Wilkinson, Alan, *Destiny: War Letters of Captain Jack Oughtred M.C.*, pp232–33

100 Wilkinson, Alan, *Destiny: War Letters of Captain Jack Oughtred M.C.*, pp231–34

101 Barnes, B.S., *Known to the Night*, p.132

102 *Hull Daily Mail*, 02/02/1917

103 *Hull Daily Mail*, 29/11/1918

104 *Hull Daily Mail*, 30/10/2014

105 *Hull Daily Mail*, 27/05/1919

106 *Hull Daily Mail*, 03/06/1919

107 *Hull Daily Mail*, 21/07/1919

108 Markham, John, *Keep the Home Fires Burning*, p.88

109 Fairfax, Ronald, *Corky's War*, pp220, 222

110 Wilkinson, Alan, *Destiny: War Letters of Captain Jack Oughtred M.C.*, p.192. Letter dated 26/06/1918

111 *Hull Daily Mail*, 24/05/1917

112 Fairfax, Ronald, *Corky's War*, p.264

113 Chapman, Peter, *Grimsby's Own. The Story of The Chums*, p.99

114 Barnes, B.S., *Known to the Night*, p.7

115 The *Hull Times*, 22/10/1927

116 Barnes, B.S., *This Righteous War*, pp159, 162. Inscription on the grave of Hull Pals man, Private Dobbs, age 21

117 Willatt, Dora.,*Thank God I'm Not a Boy!* p.154

118 Barnes, B.S., *This Righteous War*, p.137

119 Barnes, B.S., *This Righteous War*, p.65

120 Barnes, B.S., *This Righteous War*, p.143

121 Fairfax, Ronald, *Corky's War*, pp128–29

122 Babington, Anthony, *For The Sake Of Example*, p.43

123 Fairfax, Ronald, *Corky's War*, p.78

124 Dennis, Gerald, *A Kitchener Man's Bit*, pp3, 248

125 Drake, Rupert, *The Road to Lindi, Hull Boys in Africa*, p.291. Extract from diary of Dan Fewster, 1st Hull Heavy Battery RGA, being demobbed 22 January 1919

126 Barnes, B.S., *This Righteous War*, p.154

127 Sumner, Ian, *Despise It Not*, p.56

About the Author

SUSANNA O'NEILL, a former teacher, has studied the ancient cultures and traditions of Britain for many years. She is the author of *Folklore of Lincolnshire* and *The Hull Book of Days*, both published by The History Press, and lives in Hull, East Yorkshire.

BIBLIOGRAPHY

Books

Arthur, Max, *Last Post* (Cassell Military Paperbacks, London, 2005)

Avery, Alan, *The Story of Hull* (Blackthorn Press, Pickering, 2008)

Babington, Anthony. *For The Sake Of Example* (Grafton Books, London, 1985)

Baker, Esther, *A City in Flames* (Hutton Press Ltd, Beverley, 1992)

Barnes, B.S., *Known to the Night* (Sentinel Press, Hull, 2002)

Barnes, B.S., *This Righteous War* (Richard Netherwood Ltd, Huddersfield, 1990)

Bell, Robert, *Sharp Street* (Wrecking Ball Press, 2012)

Bilton, David, *Hull Pals* (Pen and Sword Books Ltd, Barnsley, 1999)

Bilton, David, *The Trench. The Full Story of the 1st Hull Pals* (Pen & Sword Books Ltd, Barnsley, 2002)

Bridger, Geoff, *The Great War Handbook* (Pen & Sword Books Ltd, Barnsley, 2009)

Census of England and Wales 1911, Vols I–II (His Majesty's Stationery Office, London, 1912)

Chapman, Peter, *Grimsby's Own. The Story of The Chums* (The Hutton Press Ltd, Beverley, 1991)

Cookson, David, *Robbie* (Highgate Publications Ltd, Beverley, 1989)

Credland, Arthur, *The Hull Zeppelin Raids* (Fonthill Media Ltd, 2014)

Davies, Richard, *Sailor in the Air* (Seaforth Publishing, Barnsley, 1967)

Dennis, Gerald, *A Kitchener Man's Bit* (Merh Books, 1994)

Drake, Rupert, *The Road to Lindi, Hull Boys in Africa* (Reveille Press, Brighton, 2013)

Fairfax, Ronald, *Corky's War* (Mutiny Press, 2008)

Gerrard, A.D., *The Road to Oppy Wood* (The Western Front Association, Hull Local History Library)

Gerrard, David, *A Century of Hull* (The History Press, Stroud, 2000)

Gibson, Paul, *Kingston Upon Hull* (Tempus Publishing, Stroud, 2002)

Gillett, Edward and MacMahon, Kenneth, *A History of Hull* (Oxford University Press, Oxford, 1980)

Goodman, David, *Aspects of Hull* (Wharncliffe Publishing Ltd, Barnsley, 1999)

Hammerton, J.A., *The War Illustrated.* Vol. 3. The Amalgamated Press Ltd, 1915

Hook, John, *This Dear Dear Land, The Zeppelin Raids on Hull and District* (London, 1995)

James, Daniel and Thomson, Ruth, *Posters and Propaganda in Wartime* (Franklin Watts, London, 2007)

Kimberley, Stephen, *Humberside in the First World War* (Local History Archives Unit, Hull, 1988)

Lake, Deborah, *Smoke and Mirrors* (Sutton Publishing Ltd, Stroud, 2006)

Markham, Alice. *Back of Beyond* (Highgate Publications, Beverley, 2010)

Markham, John, *Keep the Home Fires Burning* (Highgate Publications Ltd, Beverley, 1988)

Markham, Len, *Great Hull Stories* (Fort Publishing Ltd, Ayr, 2003)

Reckitt, Basil, *The History of Reckitt and Sons Limited* (A. Brown & Sons Ltd, 1958)

Reckitt's, *A Brief History of one of Hull's Oldest Companies* (nd)

Robinson, Robb, *Far Horizons* (Maritime Historical Studies Centre, Hull)

Russell, Stuart, *More Heroes, Villains & Victims of Hull and the East Riding* (The Derby Books Publishing Company Ltd, Derby, 2011)

Sheppard, Thomas, *To Commemorate Peace after the Great War* (A. Brown & Sons Ltd, London and Hull, 1919)

Simmons, Geoffrey, *East Riding Airfields* (Crécy Publishing, Manchester, 2009)

Slack, Cecil, *Grandfather's Adventures in the Great War* (Arthur Stockwell Ltd, Devon, 1977)

Suddaby, Steven, *Buzzer Nights: Zeppelin Raids on Hull* (nd)

Sumner, Ian, *Despise It Not* (Highgate Publications, Beverley, 2002)

Wallace, Edgar, *Kitchener's Army and the Territorial Forces* (George Newnes Ltd, London, 1915)

Wilkinson, Alan, *Destiny: War Letters of Captain Jack Oughtred M.C.* (The Hutton Press Ltd, Beverley, 1996)

Willatt, Dora, *Thank God I'm Not a Boy!* (Advanced Laser Press, Cambridge, 1997)

Williams, Edward Stanley, *In the Pink* (East Yorkshire Local History Society, 2010)

Woodhouse, D.G., *Anti-German Sentiment in Kingston upon Hull* (Hull City Council, 1990)

Wright, Trevelyan, *Voices of Hull* (Humberside Leisure Services, Hull, 1992)

Newspapers/Magazines

Hull Daily Mail
Hull Daily Mail: Flashback Decades

The Yorkshire Post
Hull Daily News
Hull Civic News
The Eastern Morning News
The Snapper, monthly journal of the EY Regiment, 1915
iContact
The Great War … I Was There!
World War 1914–1918 a Pictured History
Yorkshire Ridings Magazine
The Dalesman
The Local, Journal of the Hull and District Local History Research Group

Great War Britain: The First World War at Home

Luci Gosling

After the declaration of war in 1914, the conflict dominated civilian life for the next four years. Magazines quickly adapted without losing their gossipy essence: fashion jostled for position with items on patriotic fundraising, and court presentations were replaced by notes on nursing. The result is a fascinating, amusing and uniquely feminine perspective of life on the home front.

978 0 7524 9188 2

The Workers' War: British Industry and the First World War

Anthony Burton

The First World War didn't just rock the nation in terms of bloodshed: it was a war of technological and industrial advances. Working Britain experienced change as well: with the men at war, it fell to the women of the country to keep the factories going. Anthony Burton explores that change.

978 0 7524 9886 7